O U G H T E N
H O U S E
P U B L I C A T I O N S

"Ascension Books for the Rising Planetary Consciousness"

ALSO BY THE AUTHOR

Pathways to Self-Discovery: Tools to Help You Access Your Higher Self for Guidance and Healing, Nucleus, 1994. Available from Oughten House Publications or your local bookstore.

The Extraterrestrial Vision

Channeled Teachings from Theodore

by Gina Lake

The Extraterrestrial Vision
Channeled Teachings from Theodore

COVER ART BY DAVID ADAMS
EDITING & TYPOGRAPHY BY SARA BENJAMIN-RHODES

Published by:
OUGHTEN HOUSE PUBLICATIONS
P.O. Box 2008
Livermore, California, 94551-2008 USA

Library of Congress Cataloging-in-Publication Data
Theodore (Spirit)
    The extraterrestrial vision : channeled teachings from Theodore/
by Gina Lake.
            p.   cm.
        ISBN 1-880666-19-7 : (alk. paper) $13.50
        1. Life on other planets. 2. Spirit writings. I. Lake, Gina,
1951- .   II. Title.
    BF1311.L43T47   1994
    133.9'3--dc20   94-12461
                                                    CIP

Printed with vegetable ink on acid-free paper
Printed in the USA

CONTENTS

THE IMPORTANCE OF DISCERNMENT

In editing a book for Oughten House, I strive to take it to the highest level of which I am capable. I draw upon my intuition and experience and try to catch anything that is not accurate or clear. However, there are as many pictures of reality as there are points of awareness to formulate them. There are many destiny patterns unfolding simultaneously. We each need to use our own discernment to distinguish what is "ours" and what is someone else's. No source of information is without its distortion. Even the clearest channels are not, nor have they ever been, 100% accurate. Even within information that is "mostly true," there is some information that is not true. Even within information that is "mostly false," there is some truth present.

Your greatest ally in finding your way to your own "destination" is your own discernment. No one can know your own answers except you. You cannot rely on anyone or anything outside of you: your answers all lie within you. We are all unique aspects of the One. There is no duplication whatsoever, which is pretty amazing in itself. As you read what is in these pages, take what is "yours" and embrace it. The rest may be there for someone else. If it helps you on your path, then it has served.

— Sara Benjamin-Rhodes, Managing Editor

PREFACE

The information in this book is the viewpoint of a channeled entity on the mid-causal plane, who has evolved beyond the Earth plane and who is working to help Earth during this critical time. Undoubtedly, it is not the only viewpoint. Just as we rarely find two scientists, professors, or theologians in total agreement, we should not expect total agreement from entities or extraterrestrials about Earth's history and situation. History is colored by the historian, and this is no less true of the many entities who are trying to help us now. These more advanced entities — nonphysical and physical alike — are still evolving, as we are, and can only provide us with their version of truth from their level of understanding. So, no version of any experience is THE TRUTH; everything is subjective.

The purpose in writing this book, I am told, is to prepare us for the many changes that will result from our discovery of celestial beings. These beings will introduce themselves to us before long, and we will be faced with integrating them into our world view. The repercussions of expanding our world view to include an interactive universe will be significant, as every area of life — philosophy, religion, science, sociology, history, psychology, medicine, law, and government — will be irrevocably changed. Although we have seen change on this planet accelerate dramatically over the last fifty years as a result of technology, this is nothing compared to what will result from meeting our celestial neighbors. Humanity is about to make one of its biggest leaps ever.

The more people who understand who these visitors are, how they have been involved with us, and what their intentions are, the easier it will be to adjust to their presence. With preparation, we are more likely to have a positive outcome to such an expansion of our world view.

— Gina Lake, Spring 1993

INTRODUCTION

This book is being written to prepare you for planetary changes, the likes of which have never been experienced in humanity's history. The Earth has experienced polar shifts, ice ages, floods, and other climatic and cataclysmic occurrences. But never has humanity experienced anything like it is about to, as a result of the appearance of aliens on your planet.

"Aliens," however, is a misnomer, since you are closely related to these visitors, both genetically and spiritually. The term "aliens" also doesn't fit, because it has a negative ring to it. While most of those visiting your planet are strange looking, they are not to be feared. Most have come to help you. We will tell you who these visitors are, how they intend to help you, and how they are similar to what humanity is becoming, for in many respects, they represent your future.

Information about extraterrestrial visitors is coming through channels and psychics today, most from benevolent sources. However, be aware that not all of this information is from visitors who are trying to help you. As you will learn, some visitors are trying to undermine the good works of the many benevolent visitors. These negative extraterrestrials pose no serious threat, although they would like you to think they do. We hope to expose their activities so that they don't continue to create fear and confusion among you. They really have little power, and what they do have is quickly diminishing. Having said this, let us begin with the story of human life on your planet ...

Blessings!

— Theodore

PART 1: WHO IS HERE AND WHY

1

WHERE YOU CAME FROM AND WHERE YOU ARE GOING

YOUR ORIGINS

The information in this chapter will shock many of you. It is so controversial that you may not want to believe it. Nevertheless, it is time for you to know where you came from. Eventually, the story of your origins will be accepted, but first it will have to be introduced by many sources and in many different ways. This is just one of those sources and one of those ways.

Human beings did not evolve naturally on Earth. They evolved from genetic engineering of ape-like primates by beings visiting your Earth millions of years ago. These extraterrestrials were the first intelligent species to discover the Earth, besides one former colony of extraterrestrials that had landed here and left when your extraterrestrial forefathers/mothers arrived.

That extraterrestrials altered the DNA of certain primates on Earth to create the human species is undoubtedly shocking. And yet, your scientists are beginning to play with this same technology — "Like father, like son," you could say. Regardless of whether you approve of it or not, genetic engineering has been part of humanoid history whenever humanoids have been intelligent enough to use it.

You are only one form of humanoid. The universe is populated with many, many humanoid forms, with some basic similarities. Let's look at some of these similarities as a way of defining what we mean by humanoid. Humanoids stand erect on two legs and have (generally) two arms with various kinds of digits. They have sensing apparatuses, which vary from species to species — in your case, a nose, a mouth, skin, eyes, and ears. They also have heads, of course, in varying proportions to their bodies, all of which contain a brain or similar mechanism that rules intellectual and physical functioning. Beings that have these general physical attributes can be said to have a humanoid form. Human beings are just one species of humanoid, the one found on your planet.

The early primates on Earth had a humanoid form. However, they could not be called humanoid, because they lacked the most important ingredient of all: a soul. So, the most critical humanoid component is not physical at all, but spiritual. A soul — not just intelligence — is what separates human beings from other living creatures on Earth. No other creature on Earth except cetaceans (dolphins and whales) has an individual soul. All others have a group, or hive, soul. The soul can evolve intelligence, but intelligence, although it evolves, cannot evolve a soul. Thus, creatures on your Earth continue to evolve intelligently, but they will never become ensouled as a result. Only you and the cetaceans have this privilege and this responsibility.

The beings who colonized your planet knew this. They knew intelligence alone could not create soul. They knew the primates would not have evolved by themselves into human beings as you know them today. If humanoids were to live on Earth, they would either have to come from elsewhere and adapt to Earth or be created genetically with the help of a species already on Earth. Did you realize that even soul is encoded in the genes? It is. Everything is.

Adapting to a foreign planet, however, can take many hundreds of years and be quite painful, especially in the beginning. Such adaptation also takes a toll in lives, something that your forefathers wanted to avoid as much as possible. Therefore, they chose to create humanoids by combining their own genes with primates' genes to create hybrids. This hybridization continued for many thousands of years until the extraterrestrials could mate with the hybrids and produce offspring. At this point, the genetic engineering was stopped and evolution was allowed to continue naturally. There were many long periods in which the extraterrestrials were not actively involved in procreating with the evolving humanoids. The periods in which extraterrestrials became more involved resulted in extraordinary advances, but these periods became fewer and fewer as humankind evolved.

You may think creating life through genetic engineering is unethical. If this seems like "playing God" to you, then you are not alone. This subject is controversial even among advanced extraterrestrials. That this is a free-will universe means that anyone who invents something may use it. As with any other choice, this results in learning. You are here to learn, and in this sense, there is no such thing as a wrong choice; every choice leads to learning of some sort. From the Creator's perspective, if we may assume we understand the Creator, creating another vehicle for sentient life is not only allowed but applauded. How this is done, where this leads, and the motive for doing this is what may or may not be considered ethical.

What were the motives for creating the human species on Earth? The motives were mixed, as they would be for any endeavor that required the cooperation of many people. Many of your creators were responding to a desire for an outpost for their future reincarnating selves — another world where they could reincarnate. Others were responding to the same scientific drive and curiosity that impels much of your scientific work. While for others, this experiment — and it was an experiment, since the outcome was unknown — was a sacred opportunity to co-create with the Creator. This last group was expected to give spiritual guidance to the project.

So, although there were many motives for creating human life on Earth, the participants acknowledged the spiritual responsibility of what they were proposing and sought spiritual guidance about how to go about it. However, being fallible as they were, they did not always heed or clearly understand the spiritual counsel they received. This resulted in much learning for them. Their interactions with you today are different from what they were in the past because of what they have learned about being "gods." They will not make the same mistakes they made in the past, but they may still make mistakes!

Today you are faced with the same dilemmas they were. They questioned whether they could engineer a life form that would benefit the planet; you ask — or should ask — the same of the technology and chemicals you are creating. You cannot know how any creation will be used or how it will evolve, even though you may have specific goals in mind, because once you have created it, it is out of your hands and becomes something others act on according to their free will.

In a free-will universe, the future is hard to predict, even for advanced intelligences like your forefathers. And unfortunately, intelligence is not enough to ensure beneficial creations. The ability to create beneficial creations depends not only on the creator's intelligence but on the creator's spiritual development. The more the creator is aligned with the Creator, the more beneficial the creation will be to the Whole. On the other hand, the more out of alignment and the more intellectually advanced the creator is, the more detrimental the creation. Intellectual development does not necessarily parallel spiritual development and, in fact, often interferes with it.

We said that your forefathers sought spiritual guidance for their work. This is much to their credit, for many in the universe are not as spiritually developed as your forefathers but are still capable of genetic manipulation. Worlds have come and gone because of such individuals, who did not sense their connection with the Creator, but felt entitled to act as both creator and god to their creations. These experiments failed, and the creators (and their creations) learned. In fact, many of the creators only learned by reincarnating as their own creations! So it goes. Even the worst situations can be used to evolve us.

Service to Others and Service to Self

Your forefathers, although they were not as spiritually advanced as they are now, were still advanced enough to recognize the Creator's presence in their lives and the importance of seeking the Creator's guidance and approval for their actions. They believed in what they were doing on Earth. Their motives as a whole were to serve the Creator. This orientation toward serving the Creator is often called the path of service to others (or simply, the path of service), as opposed to the path of service to self. "Service to others" and "service to self" are names for two different approaches to evolution. Those on the path of service to others, as the name implies, believe that one returns to the Creator (evolves) by serving others. Those on the path of service to self believe that one returns to the Creator by serving oneself. They believe that in serving themselves, they are serving the Creator. Your forefathers were on the path of service to others.

These two points of view developed because the physical universe is formed around polarities: love/hate, light/dark, male/female, yin/yang, happiness/sadness. These polarities create the ground from which the lessons of physical existence arise. For instance, sadness creates a drive for happiness, and it is recognized when found because of the former experience of sadness. So sentient beings in the physical universe learn to return to God (goodness) by having the freedom to experience its opposite: self-involvement. The folly of the service-to-self path, thanks to the pain it engenders, is always eventually recognized, although sometimes only after many, many incarnations. Those who choose a service-to-self path eventually switch paths and complete their evolution by serving others.

This undoubtedly raises many questions. Do we all first choose to serve self and then change to serving others, or do we begin as one or the other orientation and then change later if we are service-to-self? Everyone begins their physical incarnations on the path of service to self and then moves either quickly or less quickly to the path of service to others. Although most do not stay long on the path of service to self, some remain there for thousands of incarnations before they decide to shift. These individuals often reincarnate together repeatedly, creating societies — whole planets — made up entirely of individuals on the path of service to self.

These worlds are a hell of sorts, but are one way for those on this path to learn that this is no way to evolve.

Eventually, they come to see the limitations of the service-to-self path. Although they may develop intellectually, psychically, technologically, and in other respects by serving themselves, a service-to-self society cannot evolve, since its members cannot function as a group. As a result, such a society does not benefit from the expertise of its members, and the members often end up using their skills against each other. Service-to-self societies are continually at war and continually overturning their leadership. If you can imagine a world without cooperation and ruled by fear, you can imagine a service-to-self world.

There are, of course, self-servers on your planet. The youngest souls, those in their first incarnations, are service-to-self. However, there is another group of service-to-self on your planet: those who have reincarnated from service-to-self worlds, who are committed to the service-to-self path. They are dangerous, because they have evolved intellectually and often psychically but not spiritually, and use their talents to advance their own ends. That they have this development and no sense of their connection to the Creator makes this service-to-self type especially dangerous.

Self-servers are as diverse as any random group of people. They work in many different professions, but are particularly drawn to ones involving power. Much of the corruption in business and government is perpetrated by self-servers, many of whom are highly intelligent. They are never found in service professions, except as impostors or con men who prey off those in need. They have no sympathy for the needy, because they believe everyone should be self-sufficient. They believe that those who can't take care of themselves will learn to take care of themselves by being taken advantage of. Consequently, they feel a spiritual duty to take advantage of the weak.

Also in this category are the Black Magicians and Satanists, who openly — or not so openly — practice the Dark Arts. Here again, their only interest is power and self-advancement. They will do anything, including murder and mutilation, to achieve their goal, which often is simply power for power's sake. Just feeling powerful is often enough for them. They achieve power by taking it away from others through control, fear, and murder. Fortunately, only a few have such grandiose dreams as taking over the world or a particular country. Those who manage to gain worldly power are likely to have spent many lifetimes on service-to-self planets like ones in the Orion constellation, where they developed their intelligence and cunning.

Another service-to-self type involved with Earth now is a group of extraterrestrials sometimes called the Greys, who are dying out because of service-to-self's inviability. This group is following somewhat of a plan, which we will say more about in the chapter on them.

One other service-to-self type involved with your planet, but also not on it, is that of multidimensional extraterrestrials from the Orion constellation, who are capable of changing form, and of materializing and dematerializing. They are working cooperatively with the Greys (at least for the time being) to undermine the transformation that others like us are trying to bring about. More will also be said about the Orions later.

These service-to-self groups and individuals are trying to create chaos on your planet now. Fortunately, as is true with all self-servers, they won't be able to maintain enough organization to make an impact on Earth's course now, although they have had an impact at different times throughout your history.

Service-to-self groups and individuals have limitations on the damage they can do, despite the intellectual and psychic development of some of them. The first limitation of service-to-self extraterrestrials like the Greys and the Orions is a self-imposed one: Out-and-out destruction of a developing race such as yours is unethical to them. That is, although they are here to take over the Earth, they will not do it by murdering you or overthrowing your governments. Instead, they are hoping to contribute indirectly to the downfall you yourselves have potentiated. They believe your destruction is inevitable, and they are positioning themselves to take over when it happens. Since they believe they have the technology to restore the environment even after a nuclear holocaust, they are not the least bit concerned that you will make the Earth uninhabitable to them — but they should be.

The Orions and the Greys are trying to hasten your downfall, stirring up trouble any way they can. Their main tactic is fear. The Greys, in particular, have announced to your government (which has been in contact with them since their landing in the late 1940s) that they will destroy you if you don't comply with their demands. Their first demand is that their presence not be revealed. This is one reason your government has been covering up its interactions with the Greys and glossing over accounts of UFOs. What your government fails to realize is that this small band of extraterrestrials does not have the technology to destroy you nor would they act so aggressively. This agreement has made it necessary for the servers to adjust their plans. The servers know the Greys' plans and their every move, and have enacted a counter plan.

The second limitation of the Greys' power is that they are physically very weak. Their life span is drastically reduced by the conditions of Earth. They have been willing to risk their lives because they believe their race will be saved through hybridization with you. But they are wrong about this. They don't have the time they need. Even genius cannot save this dying race. They don't believe this, however, and refuse to listen to advice. They are stubbornly persisting in their plan, which will lead to their demise — not yours. So we and others here to help the Earth do not see the Greys as a threat and are trying to guide them to a more successful outcome. So far, they have not listened.

Maybe knowing about the service-to-self path will help you understand why there is so much suffering on your planet. The cruelty of some people is understandably baffling to you. However, the Earth and other physical systems have always had such dramas between good and evil. Through the interplay of good and evil, you evolve. Moreover, evil evolves into good, which is the good news.

Sometime in your evolution, you will no longer need to reincarnate on a planet with this drama going on. You will eventually move beyond this and continue your evolution in nonphysical realms, in fifth density* and beyond. Your planet is going through a similar evolution, as it moves from third to fourth density. As a fourth-density planet, the Earth will still be a physical world and still evolve through polarities, but life will be easier, with much less suffering. Eventually, the Earth will evolve out of physicality into fifth density, as you will. However, that will not be for a very, very long time.

MOVING INTO FOURTH DENSITY

One reason you are being visited by extraterrestrials is that Earth is transitioning from third to fourth density, and Earth's people need help adjusting to fourth density, since it also means changing their vibratory rate. This will result in a world that operates at a higher level of consciousness. This shift is necessary, not only for Earth's survival but for it to take its proper place in the universe now.

*See Appendix for an explanation of densities.

This shift from third to fourth density is coming about more quickly than it ordinarily would. This usually takes place gradually. However, this has not happened, and now the Earth has to make a leap. The results of this shift will be astounding for everyone on Earth. Those who will not be able to withstand the change of vibration will have to leave their bodies and reincarnate where the vibration is more compatible. Unless they can make the shift to a higher consciousness, they will not return to Earth in their next lifetime.

This shift in vibration, reflected in human beings as a shift in consciousness, requires chemical changes in the body, and not everyone's body will be able to adapt. These adaptations can be eased by dietary measures, pure air and water, a peaceful environment, and meditation.

A trigger has been implanted in your DNA that will cause this consciousness shift under the right circumstances. Unfortunately, not everyone will be able to make use of the changes this trigger will release or survive in a body long enough to receive help from the trigger. This trigger was engineered within your DNA as part of the human experiment that brought you into this world. It is a precious gift from your creators, the "gods" of your ancient myths and legends. Its purpose is to ensure your survival into fourth density. More about this later.

This impending shift means that a major advance in the human race is here. Never has the Earth seen a leap in consciousness like the one about to take place. Consciousness has always evolved slowly and painstakingly, as is normal throughout the physical universe. The leap of consciousness you are about to experience is an experiment; no one is entirely sure what the results will be. What is certain, however, is that this will be a remarkable time to be on Earth.

Beings have gathered from all over to witness and participate in this transition. Both observers and guides from many corners of the universe have come. The critical issue is to what degree you will destroy Earth's environment and atmosphere before the consciousness shift takes place. A consciousness shift will not be enough, if you have already set in motion irredeemable forces of destruction. Already, much damage has occurred. One thing is clear: You — or rather your children — will pay for your environmental mistakes and shortsightedness. The only question is how much. When your consciousness shifts, although you will see the error of your ways, it will be too late to avoid certain consequences.

Although we have been trying to influence your course, we and others guiding your planet will not step in to save you from yourselves unless we have to. Our combined efforts could moderate any destructiveness. But for the most part, we will let you make your choices and live with the consequences — if it doesn't mean Earth's extinction.

Earth's Helpers

Powerful forces are at work through many of you, geared toward turning around conditions on this planet. Extraterrestrials and others here to help Earth are working through people's subconscious minds: through dreams, intuition, psychics, and channels. The message is getting across in your mass consciousness, and momentum is building toward a more positive course. In addition, many advanced souls from other planets and dimensions, often called Star People (Starseeds, or Wanderers) and Walk-ins, have reincarnated and are reincarnating on your planet to ease the shift in consciousness and guide critical choices.

Star People and Walk-ins look like ordinary people and often think of themselves as ordinary people, but they have extraordinary abilities and development. Many of the political changes occurring now are reflections of this infusion of advanced consciousness, which will not stand for oppression and which will demand democratic reform. Without the prodding of such advanced souls, such swift and monumental changes would not be possible in such a short span of time.

Changes will continue and accelerate throughout the 1990s and into the twenty-first century. The New Age is near, and although we will not venture any dates, many of you reading this will witness its arrival and experience the dramatic event that will mark it. For those who have prepared for it, this event will be most joyous. Others, who have not made the shift in consciousness and in mind, will feel fear and a sense of loss over the old order. For most of you, however, it will be cause for great celebration.

Many of the helpers (both extraterrestrial and terrestrial) are here to heal and raise consciousness, so that the triggering mechanism within your DNA will be effective. This trigger will only be tripped if you have reached a certain level of consciousness and physiological preparedness. Some work needs to be done to raise some of you to this level.

Healers are a critical part of this plan, since both physical and emotional healing are vital if the physical body is to make the vibratory shift. This is why there are so many healers now and many new types of healing being introduced. Many of the new healing techniques have been used and perfected elsewhere and brought here to help the people of Earth heal quickly.

Spiritual teachers also are important to the plan, because they can raise consciousness simply by their presence. Their other role is introducing a philosophy to uplift and nourish these times. Oddly enough, many are playing this role who would not ordinarily be thought of as spiritual teachers. Environmentalists and ecologists, for instance, are spiritual teachers of a sort, since what they are teaching is integral to the philosophical shift taking place. After all, the new world view is based on ecology and cooperation.

And then there are nonphysical entities like us, often called spirit guides, spirit teachers, or guardian angels, who have acted as guides and teachers for people on Earth throughout history. Besides working directly with people through channels and psychics, we deliver messages and promptings indirectly through dreams, feelings, the intuition, and the subconscious mind. Many of you are aware of our presence, but you don't have to be aware of us or even believe we exist for us to affect you.

Nonphysical beings have always worked with sentient life on the physical plane. Every humanoid and every sentient life form is guided every moment of its life. Beings like us are your connection to the Source, although an imperfect one, since we also are evolving. Nevertheless, we have already evolved through and beyond the physical plane and are therefore able to act as your guides and teachers. Doing this is part of our evolution and growth.

The same could be said of many of the extraterrestrials visiting you now. Many of them are spiritually advanced and can help you make choices that will lead to a better world. They differ from us in still being able to operate through a physical body. This has many advantages in helping you, as you can imagine. First, they can be seen by you when they allow it. Second, they can affect matter. So, they can act as a bridge between our world and yours. This will be particularly useful in opening up skeptical minds to spiritual realities. Extraterrestrials will give your scientists explanations for the paranormal events they have been unable to explain.

Your current scientific views will be shaken by what you will learn from the extraterrestrials. They will provide you with the missing links to your understanding, which will lead to new kinds of beneficial technology, particularly in the areas of medicine and ecology. However, just because this technology will be available in the future is no reason to continue your destructive ways. You will only be given clues to your problems, not answers. You will have to earn this technology by developing it yourselves, and that will take time, which becomes shorter the more you destroy your environment.

The service-to-others extraterrestrials visiting you now have learned much from their involvement with you over the millennia. They have learned when to interfere and when not to. This has been a hard lesson for them — and for you. A few of the Earth's worst disasters could have been avoided had they made wiser choices at certain points in your history. They are learning, as you are. Extraterrestrials are not infallible. They do not necessarily know what is best for you. That can only be determined by you, by feeling deep within yourself. Be sure not to accept any advice from them that does not resonate within you on a deep level. This is important not only because self-serving extraterrestrials will try to confuse and control you, but because one of humanity's lessons now is not giving power away to others.

Discrimination is one of the most important lessons of these times. We are not implying that service-to-others extraterrestrials will lie to you or try to trick you. But they do have their own point of view, which may not always fit for you or take into consideration your very human needs. You will, at times, have to explain your point of view and your reality to them, since they have never "walked in your shoes," although they are doing their best to understand you. So be sure to protect your own interests. Otherwise, you may end up making unhealthy compromises.

The Zetas

The service-to-others extraterrestrials visiting you now have your best interests at heart, but some of them also have reasons of their own for being involved with you. Their most basic reason for being involved with you is that they are evolving through their interactions with you. This is the spiritual purpose behind their involvement with you. Second, some of them — specifically, the Zeta Reticuli, or Zetas for short — need something only you can give them because of your genetics. This explains the experiments and abductions you've heard of, which have been going on for the last forty years.

The Zetas need your genes to re-engineer their own DNA so that they do not die out. They no longer reproduce in the usual way but through cloning, which has undermined their adaptability and, consequently, their ability to survive into the future. Therefore, the Zetas have personal as well as spiritual reasons for ensuring the human race's survival. The Zetas are particularly concerned about your fate, because they see you taking the same path they did. They, too, were more intellectually and technologically developed than spiritually developed. They, too, used their intelligence to create nuclear weapons, which in their case destroyed their planet and forced them underground. There they adapted and survived for millennia, but they did not thrive.

The poisoning of their environment, the overdevelopment of their intellect, and their adaptation to underground life resulted in their losing the ability to reproduce sexually, a problem they solved by learning to clone themselves. In spite of these remarkable adaptations, the Zetas are dying out, because they are nearly identical. Cloning does not produce the diversity that allows a species to evolve and adapt. Consequently, the Zetas are becoming weaker and weaker physically. You have the genetics they need to regain what they have lost, and they have the wisdom you need to prevent your self-destruction. In short, you need each other.

Maybe you are wondering how your genetics can possibly help the Zetas, who bear the least resemblance to you of any of the visiting extraterrestrials. First, let us say that the Zetas are the extraterrestrials who are between 3 and 4½ feet tall, with large heads and small bodies, pointed chins, large bug-like eyes, and small nondescript noses and mouths. They have spindly arms and legs, no gender, no hair, and greenish/gray complexions. These are the extra-terrestrials most commonly seen by people and known for their abductions and experiments. The other extraterrestrials don't need to interact with you as personally or as visibly and remain hidden.

The Greys, we should add, look like the Zetas, because they share the same genetics and history up to a point. They also are abducting people for the same reason as the Zetas: to save their race. The Greys, however, developed into a service-to-self race and also are here to colonize your planet.

Before today's situation can be understood, we need to look at what went on early in humanity's history, what extraterrestrials were involved, and how you were affected by them.

EARLY EXTRATERRESTRIAL INVOLVEMENT WITH HUMANITY

The Pleiadians and the Lyrans

The first humanoid race on your planet was not native to it, but came to Earth from the Lyran star system. This small band of individuals, later known as Pleiadians, came to Earth to escape conflicts on their home planet, of which they wanted no part. They were peace-loving and anxious to avoid conflict at all cost.

After settling on Earth, they experienced physical difficulties resulting from the difference in gravitation and atmosphere. To resolve this, they extracted genetic material from ape-like primates on Earth and combined it with their own DNA, which over many hundreds of years made them true terrestrials. This had no effect on the primates who contributed their genes.

Alas, the Lyrans, whom the early Earth settlers had sought to escape, found their way to Earth and began a different genetic experiment, the one we mentioned earlier in describing your beginnings. The Lyrans took up the task of creating humanoids on Earth from the same primates that had helped the first settlers adjust to Earth. The first settlers found the Lyran presence unbearable and their activities unethical, and left Earth. They traveled for generations before they finally settled in the Pleiades. Because of their important connection to Earth and their love and concern for the humanoids of Earth, the Pleiadians have been monitoring you and involving themselves in your affairs to varying degrees. We will call them Pleiadians, even though their first home was Earth.

The Lyrans lived on Earth only periodically while their humanoid creations were evolving. Remaining there for any length of time was physically uncomfortable for them, as it had been for the first settlers. They lived primarily in spacecraft, and traveled back and forth between Earth and their home planets and others with which they were involved. Their involvement with Earth increased when the humanoids they had created evolved enough to procreate with them. The first progenitors still could not live on Earth comfortably, but their offspring easily adapted to Earth and continued to procreate. Periodically, the Lyrans mixed their seed with their human offspring. These periods of infusion of extraterrestrial genes sped up human evolution exponentially.

The Lyrans spawned offspring unlike the terrestrial parent, with far greater intellectual and physical capacities, including increased size, agility, and strength. The offspring looked different from those with more terrestrial blood, although these differences lessened over time as the Lyran genes became more integrated into the human race. Height was the most outstanding evidence of the Lyrans' involvement with the burgeoning human race. Lyrans were more than seven feet tall.

Evolution this rapid created difficulties within the human race, as can be imagined. Fighting and conflict were common, as racial differences contributed to competitiveness. Certain characteristics, like tallness, light skin, and hairlessness, became more desirable than others, leaving some members of society outcast or disenfranchised. Thus, racial struggles were born early in your history and were, in fact, part of the original Lyran conflict. Your Lyran forefathers also fought over similar differences.

Enter: The Sirians

As might be expected, the Lyrans were not the only extraterrestrials interested in Earth in the early days of the human race. Millennia later, Sirians (another group that felt a claim toward Earth) arrived. Sirians were not significantly different from Lyrans in their philosophy and approach toward Earth. Sirians also felt a right — in fact, a duty — to procreate with the developing humanoid species, to lend their own genes to this developing race. There was not much the Lyrans could do about this, since they were not inclined to disallow what they, themselves, promoted. Besides, they had nothing against the Sirians. So they managed to coexist together for some time and even to cooperate in raising and guiding the human race, but not without conflict and not indefinitely.

The relationship between these two groups of extraterrestrials and the human race was that of a parent to a child. The human race was far less developed than the Lyrans and the Sirians in every respect: physically, emotionally, intellectually, socially, and spiritually. The Lyrans and Sirians created a social hierarchy to oversee the training of their charges, with themselves on top. This was not unreasonable, given the differences in development and numbers. Thus, they orchestrated the human race's social development; provided them with knowledge about agriculture, astronomy, building construction, mathematics, science, and other subjects necessary to their survival; and taught them philosophical, esoteric, and spiritual truths.

As might be expected, many of the spiritual teachings were misunderstood or purposely distorted by human beings, making their religions vacuous at best and dangerous at worst. Nevertheless, certain spiritual truths managed to survive, in part because Earth was visited periodically by advanced souls such as Krishna, Buddha, and Jesus, who came to remind people of basic spiritual truths.

Many myths, legends, and biblical stories tell of humanity's early interactions with extraterrestrials. Stories about the gods of Mount Olympus in Greek mythology reflected Lyran and Sirian leadership in that part of the world. Egyptian mythology also reflected the Sirian influence, although what has filtered down is a distorted image of these gods. The Garden of Eden is the story of humanoid creation, with the rib symbolizing the genetic exchange between extraterrestrials and early primates. And the story of Moses and the Ten Commandments and many other prophetic interactions described in the Old Testament were stories of interactions with extraterrestrials. The Old Testament, although often distorted and inaccurate, is an account of people's remembrances of the moral teachings they received from extraterrestrials, particularly from the Sirians.

Human society, history, culture, religion, and political and philosophical beliefs were all shaped by the extraterrestrials responsible for your creation. How could it be otherwise? They felt a responsibility for what they had created, and they felt compelled to share the knowledge and understanding they had gained in their own evolution. How could they create you and leave you? They felt spiritually responsible for you — and still do. Moreover, they recognize their oneness with you as spiritual beings. In short, they love you. That is why your fate is so important to them. That is why they care whether you suffer or not. Despite how arrogant and self-serving their interventions on Earth may seem, they were not. In serving you, they believed they were serving the Creator. And so they were.

Later Pleiadian Involvement

The Pleiadians did not see it this way. They did not feel comfortable with the kind of genetic engineering taking place on Earth. Because of their strong genetic, spiritual, and emotional ties with you, they felt an obligation to protect you and to oversee your evolution and the extraterrestrials' activities. They not only tried to protect you from yourselves but from the other extraterrestrials shaping you. They even intervened to balance situations they felt were out of control or which might result in damage to your species. The Lyrans and Sirians, on the other hand, were much more apt to let you make mistakes and suffer the consequences. This was a major difference between the Pleiadians and the others, a difference that was responsible for several dramas throughout your history.

Sometimes the Pleiadians did more harm than good with their interventions. For instance, the Pleiadians saw no reason for you to suffer from diseases they knew how to cure, so they gave you cures. This eased your suffering but didn't help you develop your medical knowledge. By removing the impetus for medical discovery, the Pleiadians actually delayed your intellectual growth, since the intellect is expanded by exercising it — not by being given answers or by having no need to exercise it. This is why we and others like us, and now the Pleiadians, will not give you answers to your problems. The Earth plane is a plane of polarities, and only by having difficulties and overcoming them can you evolve.

This will not change once you move into fourth density; you will simply have different challenges, ones that relate less to survival and more to fulfilling your intellectual potential. You will be less concerned with providing for your physical selves and more with providing for your intellectual and cultural selves. The fourth-density world of the future will be one in which you will be learning to function as a coordinated whole rather than as separate individuals, although your individuality will remain intact. You will be more concerned with collective good than personal good. Moving into fourth density will be a major step in humanity's evolution, as you can undoubtedly appreciate.

At the time, the Pleiadians knew this kind of interference could have such an effect, but they felt the benefits of interference outweighed the disadvantages. They had forgotten the importance of physical suffering; it had been so long since they had suffered themselves. By making this mistake, they were reminded of this. They now work to share their understanding with others who might make this same mistake.

Another mistake the Pleiadians made was to interfere in your wars. They appeared in visions to try to convince you of the irrationality of war. This had no impact, because you were too emotionally immature to negotiate. You wanted to fight. Until fighting became more painful than not fighting, fighting would continue. You have only recently become evolved enough to settle your differences nonviolently. You are open to this now because some enlightened individuals have managed to teach you peace-making skills and because you have no choice: The world is too small, and you need each other's resources.

The Pleiadians did more than just try to talk you out of fighting. At times, they physically (or not so physically) intervened to jam your weapons or foil the invention of new ones. This kind of interference is similar to what we and other spirit guides and teachers do to guide humanity. The difference is that those like us are more objective, more evolved, and have had more experience acting as guides than the Pleiadians did then. The Pleiadians have evolved considerably since then, and realize now that they were premature in playing that role with you and vow not to interfere like that anymore. They did not always have the best judgment, but their intentions were always good.

The Lyrans and the Sirians were the main players in your history, because they did not have the same compunctions about shaping you the Pleiadians had. The Pleiadians intervened only occasionally and with altruistic, protective motives, while the Lyrans and Sirians intervened regularly, out of duty as overseers of their creations. Both the Lyrans and the Sirians figured heavily in your early history. However, at a certain point, the Lyrans all but dropped out and left the task of nurturing humanity to the Sirians.

The Sirians took over until they felt humanity was ready to stand on its own. This point did not arrive until well into medieval times. Since then, the Sirians have been monitoring your activities from afar, but not appearing to you or communicating openly with you. The same is true of the Lyrans, who have been monitoring you and occasionally walking among you, but rarely intervening directly in your affairs. It is interesting, don't you think, that soon after their apparent involvement ceased, science and rationality began replacing religion.

This period of nonintervention is ending, however — not that any of these groups will intervene like they have in the past. Earth is obviously in need of help, and the Pleiadians, the Lyrans, and the Sirians are answering this call. You are, after all, their creations and members of the same galactic family.

The Sirian Role in History

Let's take a closer look at how the Sirians affected your course, since they were the key players in your history. The Sirians were your gods. The Lyrans and even the Pleiadians also played this role, but we'll focus on the Sirian role in history because they were the strongest players, especially more recently. Please understand, however, that the Lyrans and the Pleiadians have acted similarly from time to time.

The Sirians came onto the scene after the Lyrans, but they quickly took charge of the engineering of the human form. They were experts in genetic engineering, and the Lyrans stepped aside in deference to their greater knowledge. The Lyrans remained involved with you as teachers and as your gods, but appeared to you less and less frequently.

The Sirians materialized often and in many forms. Sometimes they appeared god-like: enormous, handsome or beautiful, and glowing. With this guise, how could you not assume they were gods or angels sent to rule and instruct you? More frequently, however, they reincarnated as simple shepherds, stonemasons, tailors, and the like, so that they could mingle with you and influence you in less dramatic ways. This also was a way for them to "walk in your shoes" and sample what being human is like, although their experience of being human was never really like yours. They were like gods in human form and were usually recognized as such, regardless of their garb. They could not hide their advanced development.

They also reincarnated and became prominent members of society. Many of the remarkable men and women throughout history were either reincarnated Sirians or other advanced souls. Many of the great Greek teachers — Pythagoras, Socrates, Hippocrates, and Plato — were Sirian, as were many great political leaders throughout history. Every position of power in society has been held at one time or another — usually at critical points — by Sirians. This way, they could contribute to your growth socially, culturally, and intellectually.

The Sirians continued to influence you through biological engineering as well, until they withdrew in the Middle Ages. They decided that your evolution could proceed without them after that. Besides, their attention was drawn elsewhere then.

The human race also has been greatly advanced by the periodic arrival of avatars like Christ, Buddha, Mohammed, Lao-tzu, and Krishna. However, many of their teachings have been distorted by their followers and others who did not understand the teachings, because they were not functioning spiritually on the same level as those great beings.

It was no surprise to these great beings that their teachings became distorted. They brought them knowing this would probably happen. The alternative was to leave humanity in darkness. So they arranged for others to follow them who would correct the distortions. Martin Luther and John Calvin were not avatars themselves, but fulfilled their specific mission of reform. Advanced souls like these two have reincarnated at critical points throughout history to reinstate humanity's course when necessary.

The Sirians believed firmly in letting you make mistakes so that you could learn from them. They understood that your struggles would make you stronger. Therefore, not only did they not protect you from challenges, as the Pleiadians occasionally did, but they sometimes even instigated challenges to catalyze your growth. For example, they gave you the tools by which you could destroy yourselves in Atlantis.

The Sirians were aware of the possible danger of showing you how to use atomic power, but they were willing to risk this for the technological advancements atomic energy could bring. They did not expect you to destroy yourselves; they thought you would use this energy wisely — and most of you would have. They also thought they could prevent people from misusing it, if it came to that. However, the technology got into the wrong hands and the Sirians could not prevent the disaster that followed. For this mistake, they are deeply indebted to the human race and still repaying this debt in service to your planet. In trying to catalyze your growth by introducing atomic energy, they created tremendous karma for themselves, as did those who misused this power and destroyed Atlantis.

There are many other examples like this, most with better results. Usually when the Sirians and others intervened as catalysts, they succeeded in stimulating growth, like when they gave you the technology for aerial flight. The airplane and many other equally significant innovations came from suggestions implanted within the subconscious minds of inventors, but only when such inventions were judged timely for humankind. People could have come up with these inventions earlier, had they received similar subconscious stimuli.

The Sirians and others guiding Earth now work more through the subconscious mind — through dreams, intuition, and feelings — and through channels and psychics, than more directly. They are not limited to working this way; they just choose to. Sirians have not taken on a form on your planet for a long time and probably won't. They are leaving this up to others, whom you will come to know as extraterrestrials, rather than "gods."

Who are these extraterrestrials visiting you now? We will examine five groups of extraterrestrials involved with your planet: the Pleiadians, the Sirians, the Orions, the Zetas, and the Greys. There are others — many in fact — which explains the diversity of humanoids sighted and your confusion about what is going on. Actually, only one thing is going on: You are being helped into fourth density. This is no small matter, for rarely has a planet gone through such a change so swiftly.

CATCHING UP

The reasons for the swiftness of the move into fourth density are complex and difficult to explain. Basically, humanity has fallen behind in its spiritual development. If the human race does not catch up, the Earth will transition without it. People who don't catch up won't return to Earth in their next incarnation. The Earth has been waiting for you, but it cannot wait any longer. One reason humanity has fallen behind is the absence of great spiritual leaders over the last several centuries. Since the Sirians left, you have not had the spiritual leadership you needed to keep pace with Earth's spiritual plan. And since no other extraterrestrial group stepped in to fulfill this function, you have been left without a special consciousness to guide and inspire you, although you have had intellectual geniuses. That is not enough, however. Intellectual development without parallel spiritual development is potentially dangerous, as the Zetas have discovered. You are reaching a similar point in your history, where spiritual development must catch up to intellectual development or you may destroy yourselves and your planet as the Zetas did.

Many tactics, which have already been mentioned, are being used to catch you up: extraterrestrials, spirit guides, and other nonphysical beings are working through your subconscious minds, through psychics, and through channels. And Star People and Walk-ins have reincarnated from other planets and dimensions to share their talents and wisdom with you.

Walk-Ins and Star People

Many of you have already heard of Walk-ins and will not find this idea so shocking. For those who haven't, a Walk-in is another way, besides reincarnation, to bring someone into a body. With Walk-ins, the soul "walks in" to a body of someone ready to leave the physical plane, and begins life in that body when it is vacated. Walk-ins occur, although rarely, during near-death experiences and other serious illnesses that are followed by "miraculous" recoveries. Let us repeat that this phenomenon is rare, but less so now than in nearly any period in history.

Walk-ins have been used at other critical points in history, but this is one of the more drastic measures for rescuing planets or races. This intervention is not used casually, because it is considered best to let races evolve as they will. This is a serious intervention, because it brings in souls who will reshape the choices being made by the faltering race. It is considered an interference into a race's evolution, but one that will be made when extinction is an issue. That there are many Walk-ins on your planet now should tell you something about the seriousness of your situation!

Every Walk-in and Star Person has his or her own specific mission. They are not coordinated to perform one certain function on Earth. Some Walk-ins and Star People are working together on projects, but the projects are diverse. Some are working on environmental issues, some are involved in politics, some are trying to change your educational system, some are involved in the media, and many are healers.

What is true of all of them is that they are on the fore-front of what they do, for they have come to change existing conditions. If you look around you, you can spot them. They are the ones pushing for change in health, education, the environment, human rights, animal rights, and other New Age areas. Walk-ins and Star People are decidedly New Age, for lack of a better term. They are all healers: healers of people, of social institutions, of political hatreds, and of all life on this Earth.

Although their method for obtaining a body is unusual, Walk-ins are not more unusual than Star People. Both are extremely diverse, as they encompass individuals from many different planets and dimensions. Consequently, much variance exists among these groups in their abilities and in their level of development. Star People and Walk-ins are anywhere from (as spiritually developed as) Earth's oldest souls to (as developed as) avatars like Jesus.

Star People and Walk-ins do not necessarily strike people as being this spiritually evolved, because many haven't awakened to their true consciousness yet. Those who have are aware of how different they are. They have difficulty being accepted by ordinary people, who find them strange. This will change as the planet's consciousness changes. Thus, there are many advanced souls walking on your planet who are expressing only a fraction of their true consciousness and using only a fraction of their gifts. The times have not allowed this to be otherwise.

Many of you are probably wondering what being a Walk-in or a Star Person is like, and whether you are one. Star People and Walk-ins do not necessarily know who they are, although they are likely to realize this sometime. Besides having a sense of being different, most Star People and Walk-ins have unusual abilities. Some have these abilities even as children, but more often they develop when they are older, either rapidly or slowly. Many psychics and channels on your planet today are Star People or Walk-ins, with Star People being much more common.

The Star Person's or Walk-in's growing sense of being different and the development of unusual abilities eventually culminate in a sense of mission and purpose. At some point, whether or not they have heard of Star People or Walk-ins, they just know who they are and what their mission is. When they do discover that Star People and Walk-ins exist, which usually happens after searching for others like them, they feel immense relief. Fortunately, these days, plenty of information is available for those looking for explanations for their odd feelings. Most Star People and Walk-ins are naturally drawn to the New Age movement and find their answers there. The New Age movement has been aware of the phenomenon of Star People and Walk-ins for well over a decade.

Like Star People, Walk-ins are not immediately aware of where they came from or how they got here. When Walk-ins first awaken to their new life on this planet, they awaken as the person whose body they inhabit. They have all the memories and abilities of that person, but sense that they have been transformed, which is often attributed to their brush with death. This brush with death is seen as a turning point in their life. They see their old self as having ended at that point and a new self as having emerged. Most Walk-ins throughout history never realized what happened. But these times will be different, as more and more Walk-ins are introduced to this idea through books and other means. Extraterrestrials, nonphysical beings, Star People, and Walk-ins have the same goals and often work together. So we cannot talk about the extraterrestrials' involvement with Earth, without also mentioning these other groups and how they interact.

Nonphysical and Extraterrestrial Helpers

Before going into this, it might be helpful to clarify who we are and who we mean by "nonphysical beings." Nonphysical beings include fifth-density beings (spirit guides and others on the higher astral plane), sixth-density beings (spirit teachers and others on the causal plane, the plane beyond the astral), and seventh density beings (beings on the buddhic plane, the plane beyond the causal). We are a sixth-density entity on the mid-causal plane, where both teachers for people on Earth and guides to spirit guides can be found.

Just as spirit guides are assigned to each of you, we are assigned to watch over the work of several spirit guides. We teach them how to improve their work with people. We are particularly involved with spirit guides who are working with Star People and Walk-ins, since their work relates most to Earth's transformation. Similarly, seventh-density beings oversee the work we sixth-density beings are doing.

We are working with the extraterrestrials to help them create a plan for Earth that fits the Creator's intentions for Earth. We work with them like your souls work with you in formulating a life plan before being reborn. Thus, the extraterrestrials are evolving through their interactions with you, and we help them make choices in keeping with your highest good. This is how they are learning about being "gods" to you. They evolve by interacting with you and by nurturing your civilization.

Extraterrestrials are fourth-density (physical) and beyond (nonphysical). There is no difference between fifth- and sixth-density extraterrestrials and fifth- and sixth-density spirit guides and teachers. We only make this distinction because you experience some beings as extraterrestrials, with spacecraft and other paraphernalia (some of which they materialize), and others (like us) as spirits.

Like us, extraterrestrials are involved with Star People, Walk-ins, and others psychically and through intuition and dreams. Unlike us, however, extraterrestrials on occasion interact physically with people. But mostly, extraterrestrials act like spirit guides, implanting ideas into people's subconscious minds and dreams, and communicating psychically and through channeling to those who are receivers. And, like spirit guides, they accompany certain people on out-of-body visits to other planets and dimensions, where they are given knowledge and understanding useful to Earth's plan.

Few people remember these astral travels, but even if they don't, they are affected on deep levels. These travels speed up their evolution. This is why old souls, who can astral travel, evolve much more quickly than younger souls. A great deal is learned on these astral visits that applies to the traveler's personal life, as well as to his or her mission on Earth.

Star People, Walk-ins, and others on Earth make prelife agreements to help each other. So they, too, are working together. Some are conscious of working with others toward certain goals, but many help each other unconsciously and without ever meeting each other. For example, one person may publish the findings of a study someone else needs. No one is working alone. Everyone is involved with other people, spirit guides, spirit teachers, and extraterrestrials. Everyone is working together to bring about the plan for Earth, a plan in which everyone plays a part.

Many of you believe that there are realms beyond the physical, but few of you have had experiences with these realms or with the beings we have described. Few of you have seen or spoken to an extraterrestrial, a spirit guide, or a spirit teacher. But even if you have never had an experience of these beings, being open to the possibility that they exist makes it more likely that you will benefit from their help. Those of you who believe extraterrestrials exist, either consciously or unconsciously, are the ones they are likely to work with, either consciously or unconsciously.

CONTACTEES

You are probably wondering why some people are contacted and not others, and if people can request contact. Everyone who is contacted (physically or nonphysically) has made a soul-agreement to be contacted. They have made this agreement not only because it stands to benefit Earth's plan, but because it will benefit their own growth, as well. So, these contacts serve not only Earth's evolution, but the contactee's also.

Many of these contacts are for service: that is, the contactee has agreed to be contacted to serve Earth's plan. However, there is more to be gained by the contactee than the satisfaction of service. Contactees are evolved through their contacts with extraterrestrials, even when these contacts are nonphysical. Contactees are exposed to a higher vibration of energy that raises their consciousness, often serving to awaken them to their Star Person or Walk-in identity and mission. This awakening, in turn, creates enormous changes in their personal lives and attitudes. So, they are not only evolved spiritually but emotionally by their contacts, with many contactees resolving difficult karmic patterns in record time. Contactees have agreed to undergo exceptional experiences to evolve quickly. That is their personal karma in this.

Will someone be contacted if he or she asks to be? Extraterrestrials can pick up such signals, but they won't always respond to them. More than just a conscious desire for contact is needed; the contact also must fit the spiritual plans of everyone involved. This means the contact must fit not only the person's spiritual plan, but the extraterrestrial's, as well. If an extraterrestrial is not available whose plan fits the kind of contact needed, then contact will not be made. On the other hand, if a spiritual agreement can be made, then the contact will be pursued.

Extraterrestrials are contacting people in greater numbers than ever before. The most common type of contact, as we have said, is through the subconscious mind by way of dreams, astral travel, the intuition, feelings, and psychic means. Through these means, extraterrestrials convey their vision — their plan for Earth. They convey different pieces of the picture to different people, depending on the role the contactee has agreed to play before being born. You see, as unbelievable as it may seem, each of you — not only contactees — has made a pre-life agreement to play a role in the important drama of these times. People have always made such choices before incarnation, but these times have demanded agreements specific to the transformation. No one is insignificant in this plan;

everyone has a part. Consequently, fulfilling one's part is very important.

People also are being contacted physically by extraterrestrials. The most common way is by what you have called abduction, in which people are taken aboard spacecraft. Another way is by visitation, in which extraterrestrials appear only briefly before someone, usually to deliver a message. The third way is by sightings, in which craft and possibly their passengers are spotted briefly. These three types of physical contact serve three distinct purposes. Let's look at each.

Abductions

Abductions are the most controversial type of contact. They have been called abductions because of how you experience them. However, every person ever abducted has given his or her permission on a soul level. Therefore, from a higher perspective, "abduction" is not the right word; "fulfillment of an agreement" would be more accurate. Nevertheless, we'll continue to use this term, since you are used to it.

Most abductions are for advancing the extraterrestrials' understanding of Earth life and human beings, and for retrieving genetic material for their work. Abductions never happen without a purpose. The same could be said about the other types of contact: When UFOs or extraterrestrials reveal themselves or allow themselves to be seen, it is always for a reason.

As many of you are aware, some abductions are for retrieving DNA or eggs, or for inseminating a female. This is part of the genetic engineering between your species and the Zetas, who are trying to save their race and ensure the human race's preservation, should human beings destroy themselves through nuclear holocaust. They are saving your sperm and ova and other genetic material to ensure your re-creation in case you need to be duplicated sometime. They are doing this out of love and concern for the human race.

They also are creating a hybrid race from their own genetic material and yours to help them regain the ability to reproduce and adapt, which they have lost. If you recall, the Zetas poisoned their world and were forced to adapt to underground life, where they lost the ability to reproduce sexually. They want to go backwards in time genetically. They have come to you, because your genetics are their lost genetics.

They also are studying you, because if they are to become more like you through genetic engineering, they need to understand your emotions. Through genetic engineering, they eliminated their emotional responses, because they believed then that their emotions caused the destruction of their planet. However, this made it harder for them to evolve, since the design for humanoid growth in this sector of the universe is to evolve via the emotions. In doing this, they eradicated the means by which their species evolves. They didn't realize that their unchecked intellectual development, or rather, intellectual development unmatched by spiritual development, was the real culprit.

You could say that every mistake the Zetas made was a result of intellectual development without spiritual understanding. They were playing God even with themselves, and they discovered they were not up to the task. They have learned a great deal since then. Therefore, they have come to give you a most urgent message: "Don't make the mistakes we did." They see you as themselves long ago. They see you might make the same choices they did. They fervently hope you don't.

As part of their study of you, they are studying your glandular secretions, since they are tied to emotions in your species. They now understand the relationship between the body and the emotions, but how the emotions work interpersonally remains a mystery to them, and one fraught with discomfort. They are very uncomfortable with your emotions. Deeply imbedded within them is the judgment that emotions are primitive and destructive. This is something they will have to overcome as a race if they are to regain the benefits of being emotive.

The Zetas are mere shadows of yourselves, although highly intelligent ones. This is clear to those of you who have met them. They are efficient, emotionless, and unindividuated. What you'll gain from meeting them is an appreciation for the human population's diversity. After meeting them, you'll find it easier to celebrate your differences.

The extraterrestrials also are studying the damage you have done to the Earth and its ecology. With certain tests, they are gauging the seriousness of the damage. This is essential in understanding the future effects of this damage and what it will take to return the environment to a healthier state. Your scientists are not the only ones who cannot agree on how serious the damage is. Extraterrestrials and others guiding your planet also cannot agree. Some think you have doomed the planet to centuries of repair, while others are confident the Earth will mend more quickly than that. One thing is certain: The next century will demand significant adaptations by human beings, flora, and fauna.

The most serious danger is yet to come, since it relates to global warming and the loss of the Earth's protective ozone layer. The holes in the ozone, apparent even now, will not shrink nor global warming be curtailed until you drastically reduce your production of CFCs, reforest your planet, and stop using fossil fuels, none of which will happen soon enough to prevent a worsening of these conditions.

If you think global warming will be a sunny picnic, may we remind you that a temperature change of even a few degrees can drastically change the climate throughout the world, with deserts becoming flooded and breadbaskets becoming barren. Have you any idea what this will do to the world's economies? The face of the planet will change profoundly over the next fifty years because of what you have already done. And still you continue to heap more damage on an already ailing planet!

The extraterrestrials have some technology that can help you neutralize some of the poisons you have dumped into the environment. They have advice to give you about what to stop doing and what to do more of, they have ways of purifying your water and food, and they can show you ways of producing food that do not require danger- ous chemicals or gas-consuming vehicles. They will help you develop a clean energy source. However, you will still have to live with what you have created on Earth — if you still can, which is where the debate comes in. Human beings are very adaptable, but adaptation is not easy. As men- tioned earlier, adapting to a foreign environment can be painful, which is essentially what you will have to do in the twenty-first century. The next generation will not have it any easier, since they also will have to adapt. They will not be born adapted to the environment you have created. Many of today's children won't be able to have children, as sterility will be widespread because of the buildup of contaminants in your food and water. The population will be seriously reduced over the next decade for many reasons, and the people remaining will have difficulty reproducing. This puts you in a position like the one the Zetas found themselves in millennia ago, when they destroyed their planet with nuclear explosions. Even without massive nuclear explosions, you have defiled your planet to a critical point, one that will greatly reduce your viability as a species.

Did you realize the situation was this critical? Undoubtedly not, or you would have done something about it. That is always the problem. The Zetas did not realize how critical their situation was either, until it was too late. However, this will not be allowed to happen to Earth. It may be late, but it is not too late. Those here to help Earth will see to it that Earth and human beings are spared, or at least preserved to some degree.

So those of you who have come here to help have a big task. You will not be able to sit by and watch yourselves self-destruct. Many of you have come from places that did just that, which is one reason you are here now. You have a karmic duty and a drive to see that this civilization doesn't do the same. So, races learn from their mistakes and help others as payment for their mistakes and as service to other races. If you are wondering where the helpers were when the Zetas destroyed their planet, the answer is that the helpers were not heeded. So it goes, in a free-will universe. You have the free will even to destroy yourselves. Let's hope you don't exercise that freedom.

Visitations

Like abductions, visitations serve a purpose too. Visitations occur to remind those who have soul-agreements with the extraterrestrials of these agreements. Often those visited are asked to do something to help the extraterrestrials. Visitations are becoming more frequent and will increase as the time for a rendezvous approaches. They are not only preparing people for their role in the plan, but for a more formal meeting with them. The more people contacted before they contact you more formally, the less shocking the announcement of their presence will be. In fact, the extraterrestrials will not contact you more formally until most of the population is used to the idea of their presence. Visitations are preparing everyone for this inevitable rendezvous.

Occasionally, visitations are made spontaneously when an opportunity arises, but always with the soul-agreement of those involved. Most of these types of visitations are for exposing random people to the extraterrestrial presence and occur to people who are likely to be believed. During spontaneous visitations, little is communicated and the person or persons visited are left with many unanswered questions. This is the extraterrestrials' intent. They are not ready to reveal their purpose yet — only their presence. Revealing their purpose will come later, in a more formal meeting with your governments when the time is right. Until then, they offer only bits and pieces of information and answer questions only briefly.

UFO Sightings

The UFO sightings serve a similar purpose in preparing people for a more formal meeting. The extraterrestrials are allowing themselves to be seen more and more frequently as a way of introducing themselves to you. By showing themselves to you all over the globe in their various sizes and shapes, they are saying, "We are here; we are many; we don't all look alike; we have advanced technology; and we are peaceful." These are important messages, for although they can communicate with you telepathically and by other means, there is no guarantee you will trust what they say.

By coexisting with you in their own way over the past fifty years, they are demonstrating their peaceful intent. The many messages they have given people during their visitations and abductions also confirm their good will. However, they know that actions speak louder than words, so their main strategy has been to win your trust through their actions. Unfortunately, certain extraterrestrials, namely the Greys, have been undermining the trust they are trying to establish. We will say more about them in their own chapter.

WHAT LIES AHEAD

Before closing this chapter, we want to make a few points about the significance of these times. You have learned that your race is on the brink of destruction. You would never be in this mess if you were not living from third-density consciousness. So, the solution is to raise your consciousness. This will not be enough, however. Yes, it will stop the destruction, because you will make different choices. But you have already set in motion damages that will not disappear with a shift in consciousness. The damage, which could make Earth uninhabitable to you, higher consciousness or not, must be repaired. You have set in motion circumstances that will change the climate and the land masses. If this doesn't make Earth uninhabitable, it will at least turn economies upside down and unsettle your societies. Yes, we have every faith you will eventually reestablish more humane and ecologically sound communities. However, we also are deeply concerned about the short-term, as you should be.

If Earth's overall temperature increases appreciably, the distribution of water on your planet will change. Whether you realize it or not, civilization is now, and always has been, founded on the availability of water. As human beings, you need water. In times to come, you will realize the importance of water to civilization, to productivity, to health, and to well-being. Not only will you realize your water is limited, but that it is poisoned. Extraterrestrials can help you with this dilemma; but they cannot instantaneously rebuild your socioeconomic structures, cure those whose bodies are already full of contaminants, and make you live in peace with each other — although they will try.

Raising your consciousness is essential if you are to change your ways and lead happy lives amidst the travail of the coming decades. Raising your consciousness will allow you to live with peace, kindness, hope, and determination to build a better world. Without a shift in consciousness, the next decades would be full of misery. With a shift in consciousness, they will be enlightening. So, we are not contradicting ourselves when we speak of a coming Golden Age or of a better world even in the near future. Even in the near future, the world will be infinitely better in many respects.

In times to come, you will live by spiritual values again. In your pain, you will come to know God as you have never known God. You will see the role pain plays in your happiness and how it serves your growth. Happiness is not born from money or fame or even ease, but from experiencing the richness of life, which may not be possible until you have lost what you love. In losing what you love — pure water, clean air, animals, trees — you will come to appreciate the preciousness of these things. Regaining them will make you all feel like kings.

During this time of challenge and transformation, you will be given the spiritual understanding you need to see the silver lining of this cloud. You will be given the strength and the hope you need, because you will be given a vision of what is to come, a vision in which you all can believe and for which you all will be willing to work. This vision of a new life — a new world — will be the essence of your happiness in the times ahead. In many respects, that will be all you will have after losing your old way of life. The next five chapters describe in greater detail who is here to help and who is here to hinder, and what their immediate plans are. We cannot give you specifics of their plans or what they have already done, however. The specifics are not for you to know yet. What we will tell you is what you can know so far about the extraterrestrial situation, a situation that is unfolding every day. The closer you get to the inevitable meeting with extraterrestrials, the more you will be able to know about their plan — their vision. For now, we will tell you only as much as we can.

THE PLEIADIANS

The Pleiadians, being the first visitors to Earth, were important to Earth and the events that would later occur there. Because they became terrestrial, a special bond with Earth was formed, a bond they honor to this day. The Pleiadians did not take their stint on Earth lightly for several reasons. The first is that it was more than a stint — it lasted thousands of years and changed them as a race. It marked a special period in their history, of much growth and sacrifice.

To leave Earth as they did was the ultimate sacrifice. This meant leaving the only planet that those alive had ever known as home. It meant they would have to find another planet and adapt to it, a formidable and consuming task. And it meant being adrift in space for an unknown amount of time, all the while not knowing what would become of them. This takes its toll on a race, and when this happens, it is rarely forgotten or minimized in its history. So it was with the Pleiadians. Along with their memories of Earth are the memories of hundreds of years in space in search of a new home.

One reason this was such an ordeal is that they had already adapted to Earth's environment, an environment that is unique in this corner of the universe. Finding another planet like Earth was not easy, and they were not willing to undergo more genetic adaptations. They searched until they found a planet where they could live comfortably.

While this wandering was taking place, others in this group continued to act as scouts to Earth. They relayed information about the Lyrans' progress with the developing humanoids: you. They were disheartened to hear that the Lyrans had followed through with their plans to create your species. They felt the Lyrans were playing God at your expense and were not up to the task. They didn't approve of this kind of genetic engineering, because they didn't think anyone living within a physical dimension was evolved enough to do this responsibly.

You could say the Pleiadians were a cautious bunch. They knew that remarkable, often painful, growth can come from being a creator, and they were not willing to expose themselves or their creations to this pain. They believed in evolving with as little pain and conflict as possible. This was one of their most deeply held beliefs, one they had upheld ever since they left the Lyran system. This belief distinguished them from the other Lyrans. It became a badge they wore proudly.

Since that time, they have learned to see things differently, which is painful for them to admit. They have learned the benefit of conflict and pain, but they are still intrepid pioneers in this area. Embedded within them still is a feeling that conflict and pain are wrong. This prevents them from being more courageously aggressive toward life. These feelings are reflected collectively as a tendency toward surrender and adaptation rather than aggression and forcefulness.

This tendency to adapt or surrender to challenges rather than push through them, they have since learned, has inhibited their evolution and resulted in stagnation. Their tendency has been to maintain existing conditions or leave and re-create them elsewhere, rather than venture into the unknown. This is apparent even in their not settling on a planet until they found one like Earth. Change is not their strong suit, and this is because they have avoided conflict and pain whenever possible.

However, as we have said, this is changing. At least intellectually, they now appreciate the value of conflict and pain, even though their instincts still tell them to avoid these things. This conflict between instincts and the intellect causes them fear and guilt. This is something with which the Pleiadians, as evolved as they are, are still struggling. Their feelings of fear and guilt are not the same as yours, but similar.

When we say the Pleiadians are more evolved than you, we mean two things. First, they are more intellectually developed. They use about 50% more of their brains than you. Their more highly developed right brain also makes them more intuitive, creative, and psychic than you. As you can imagine, their expanded intellectual capacity enhances their ability to survive. In fact, survival is not an issue for them. They have developed technology that supports their physical needs without damaging their resources. Consequently, everyone in their society has their basic needs met with a minimum of effort, allowing time and energy for other things.

The Pleiadians have occupations like you, but they are occupations of choice, not of necessity. Everyone is asked to give something to society. There are no restrictions or limitations on how this is done. The only criterion is that one's work contributes to society. Disputes about this are rare, since the Pleiadians have clearly defined social values and goals, another reflection of their evolvement. As your brain capacity expands, you too can look forward to expanded intellectual powers and harmonious relationships.

Your race is likely to make substantial intellectual strides over the next century, so much so that your civilization will not look the same by the end of the twenty-first century. This should not surprise you, given the changes you have seen in this century. However, those in the next will be even more profound. Even your physical appearance will change, as certain mutations occur and advances are made in genetic engineering, cosmetic surgery, and medicine. Such a marked change in appearance is something your race has not experienced since its beginning and infancy.

Pleiadians also are more evolved than you spiritually, which has emotional and social ramifications as well. As a result, they are more detached from their egos and their emotions. They still have them, but they are not ruled by them but by their Higher Self. They are aligned with the aspect of themselves that knows God and they make their choices from that aspect, rather than from their ego-self.

In their race, the ego has degenerated — at least this is how it seems from your perspective. What has happened to the ego in their society is similar to what has happened to the instincts in yours. The ego has become something that is useful but not that relevant. They view the ego as a remnant of their more atavistic self, which they honor but which they recognize is not their True Self. Most people, on the other hand, still believe they are their egos and only occasionally recognize the God-Self.

Because the Pleiadians have a different relationship to their egos, they have a different relationship to each other. This also affects their social systems. The ego is what pits one person against each other. When the ego is recognized for what it is, competition gives way to cooperation. Competition cannot exist when people know the truth about who they are. The Pleiadians know that everyone comes from one Source. Moreover, they have experienced that Source, so they can't help but follow the Golden Rule.

Can you imagine a society that lives by the Golden Rule? Such a blessed state is hard to imagine — but try — since that is the state to which you are evolving. That is what you have to look forward to in your future societies, not that everything will be perfect. Utopia doesn't exist — not on the physical plane, anyway, although the planes beyond the physical come closer and closer to perfection. Still, perfection is neither the state of the physical nor the nonphysical universe. Change and evolution is, and perfection is too static a concept to fit this scheme. Perfection implies an end point, and evolution and creation have none.

The Pleiadians are not a perfect society: they have their problems. Their discomfort with conflict and pain is their biggest one. This includes discomfort with their own negative feelings, which they are not beyond having. The Pleiadians go to great lengths to avoid negativity, even to the point of stifling creativity.

For example, if a Pleiadian has plans for inventing a new vehicle, he will have to submit them to a committee for approval. He will have to show that it will benefit society and how he will counteract any harm it might create. However, all this must be based on figures, since the invention cannot be built without the committee's approval. If it turns out different from what was presented to the committee, it will have to be reevaluated. If it doesn't pass the committee's standards, it will be scrapped and the inventor will have lost whatever time and effort he invested in it.

If your society had such a committee, it would have rejected the Wright brothers' work and every other twentieth-century invention because of their potential to damage the environment. As a result, you would not have evolved technologically. This is what has happened in Pleiadian society. They have made minute strides in science and technology, compared to other societies at their same level. This doesn't bother most of the Pleiadians. Most agree they prefer a society that puts social welfare above techno-logical progress.

Still, there is another problem with this. In not allowing themselves to be challenged by questionable enterprises, the Pleiadians have eliminated many of the factors that stimulate personal and spiritual growth. They have all but eliminated the negative pole. Although their society may seem advanced spiritually, it is not as advanced as it could be. By avoiding the challenges that come with a free society, they have stunted even their spiritual growth.

The Pleiadians are learning to balance individual freedom with the good of society. Right now, the good of society is emphasized. Many other societies have erred in the opposite direction — yours, for example. Eventually, the Pleiadians will shift more to the other pole. They are striving to do this, but morally such freedom is still repug-nant to them. In every society, evolution is born from this struggle between the individual and society. But it happens much more slowly in a society that emphasizes society's welfare over individual freedom.

Maybe you are thinking that it would have been better if there had been no technological development in the twentieth century, given the destruction it has caused the Earth and native peoples. What this point of view does not acknowledge is that you are learning an important lesson by facing the results of your actions. What you are learning now will prevent you from ever making this mistake again in your future lives. You will get through this period, the Earth will be restored, and because of what you have learned, you will build a more humane society with more humane technology.

If you had never made these choices, you would not have had the opportunity to learn this valuable lesson and move beyond this stage in your growth. Preventing you from making these choices would have kept you from evolving beyond them. You would have remained stuck at a certain level of evolution. This is what has happened to the Pleiadians. They recognize this now and are challenged to change. Their choice also led to learning, but it slowed their evolution as well.

Pleiadians look like you, at least those of you who are Caucasian. This should not be surprising, when you consider your origins and Pleiadian history. Pleiadians are Lyrans with early Earth-primate genes, and you are a combination of Lyran and early Earth-primate genes as well. You are more diversified in appearance than Pleiadians because of the mixing of Sirian and other genes into your species as it evolved. This, in addition to adapting to a variety of climates, created your races. If you saw a Pleiadian, you would never guess that he or she was not from Earth. This is why they have been chosen to introduce the extraterrestrial situation to you when the time is right.

One way Pleiadians are different from you is that they are all attractive. This is because they have evolved beyond the need to experience being unattractive, something that serves an important function early in a species' evolution. Being unattractive teaches compassion for physical differences and the superficiality of outer beauty. Once these lessons are learned, a species no longer needs to be born into unattractive bodies (or ones a society considers unattractive). Despite their attractiveness, Pleiadians do not all look alike. Their population has as much variation as any of your races.

Pleiadians in some respects are your future selves. They have represented one of your probable futures biologically and spiritually, but so far not socially and emotionally. You and the Pleiadians have taken separate paths emotionally. You are open to conflict and pain, and acknowledge your negative emotions, while they do not — or have not. Therefore, you have been developing differently emotionally. Given that the Pleiadians are acknowledging their negativity more, your future and theirs (emotionally and socially) are likely to be more similar.

The Pleiadians will play a crucial role in introducing you to the extraterrestrial mission. Because they look like human beings, they are best suited to approach your government and others with the extraterrestrials' offer of help. The drawback of this plan is that the Pleiadians may not be believed, since they look like ordinary human beings. If this happens, other proof has been arranged. What's important to the extraterrestrials is that they not send you into a panic or cause a war. They realize that the stranger they look, the greater the likelihood of a negative outcome.

The Pleiadians have been monitoring Earth from a large mothercraft, which has been circling Earth for millennia. This mothercraft is not visible to you, because it is in outer space and can avoid satellite and other detection by shifting out of the third dimension. Avoiding your detection is no challenge for them. On this mothercraft are hundreds of Pleiadians, all with specific tasks pertaining to their terrestrial mission. This mission consists of helping you make the transition from third to fourth density, with everything this entails. The Pleiadians are especially skilled at negotiation and peacemaking, which is another reason they will be the ones to approach you. They will offer you their mediation skills.

The Pleiadians also are pledged to help the Zetas in their genetic work. They are not guiding the Zetas' work, only helping them out as needed and following their directions. Most human-looking beings spotted by human beings on spacecraft during abductions are Pleiadian helpers, although sometimes an actual human being — usually a Star Person or a Walk-in — also is aboard to help.

While they are sleeping, Star People and Walk-ins are often drafted to help the extraterrestrials. Star People and Walk-ins come aboard the spacecraft in their astral form, which appears solid to abductees under these conditions. Many of the abductees also are taken aboard spacecraft in their astral forms rather than in their physical bodies. This accounts in part for their not being able to recall their extraterrestrial encounters.

The Zetas also are being helped by a variety of other extraterrestrials not described in these pages. From all over the universe, the Zetas have gathered the expertise they need to accomplish their complex and demanding task. This explains the diversity of extraterrestrial life forms reported by abductees. This is no different from you assembling the best scientific minds from around the world to work on a specific project. You don't work this way yet, but when you do, science will make tremendous leaps. It is ironic that science has been used to defend yourselves from each other when its real value lies in uniting and improving the world for everyone.

The Pleiadians are operating from a central command station on their mothercraft, called the Ashtar Command. One of them is Commander Hatonn. Hatonn has been in communication with several channels for some time. However, a group of negative Sirians are impersonating Hatonn, which has caused much confusion. This Hatonn impersonator is spreading a message of fear and doom through written materials he has dictated.

This is typical of the negative extraterrestrials' activities. Their primary purpose is to undermine faith in your government and hasten the decline they believe is inevitable. This imposter has dictated a large body of information that describes conspiracy, economic decline, and the destruction of your planet. We and the positive (service-to-others) extraterrestrials do not hold his views on conspiracy and doom, although you *are* coming very close to destroying yourselves.

The idea that a worldwide conspiracy exists that is both diabolical and invincible is an idea that only self-servers would cook up and only service-to-self planets have *ever* managed to manifest. This is one of their favorite ploys. They have used it on other planets throughout their history, and now they are using it on you. Fortunately, it rarely works because self-servers lack the organization — not to mention the numbers — to imprison races with these ideas. This plot has only been successful on service-to-self planets, not on ones that have as many servers as yours. For as difficult and ugly as life gets on your planet, Earth is a heaven compared to the hell of a service-to-self planet.

The service-to-self extraterrestrials are trying to undermine your confidence in your government and in your future. This is a clever move, because there is reason to doubt your government and your future. This is what makes their work so insidious. They are saying the same thing we are — that the world is in dire straits. The major difference is in how they are saying it, what they see as the outcome, and why they are saying it. Their messages are designed to instill fear and a sense of powerlessness. They hope to shock, frighten, and paralyze you, all under the guise of trying to help and mobilize you. However, underneath their words is the clear message: "You don't have a chance."

Fortunately, once you understand the difference in communication styles between negative and positive extraterrestrials, negative extraterrestrials are easy to spot. Do you feel frightened, shocked, and overwhelmed by the message? Do you feel it is too late, that the powers of destruction are too great? Is there a tone of dogmatism in the message? For instance, do they claim to have the truth and demand that you accept it — or else? These are all signs of service-to-self.

You also can tell whether a message is from a positive or a negative source by how it makes you feel. Messages from negative extraterrestrials leave you feeling bad. Granted, you may not feel uplifted by everything we are saying, but our message as a whole is hopeful. Besides, we don't demand that you accept it. You should come away from an extraterrestrial message feeling hopeful and inspired to take positive action.

Messages from negative extraterrestrials give you no positive course to follow. They suggest you save yourself (build bomb shelters, protect your money supply, store food and water). How like self-servers to emphasize what you can do to save yourself, rather than what you can do to help the world or others! Here again, this information is insidious, because being prepared for food and clean water shortages (we do not foresee nuclear holocaust, as they do) is not unwise. However, to emphasize this as a course of action is to encourage you to withdraw your energy from doing something to solve your problems. This is what they want you to do. They don't want you to work together to solve the problems plaguing Earth. They want you "looking out for number one." They know that will hasten your downfall. How ironic that they don't see how looking out for number one is causing their own downfall.

The Pleiadians and others are observing the negative extraterrestrials' tactics without interfering with them or countering them. This might seem odd to you, but they believe in allowing individuals to operate freely so that learning can take place on both sides. The negative extraterrestrials will not learn from their mistakes if they are not allowed to make them, and neither will you. In this free-will universe governed by polarities, such activities are allowed, at least for a time. The positive extraterrestrials will allow the negatives to continue as long as they don't upset their plan. As it is, they are merely causing some confusion and fear.

One of your biggest lessons during these times will be discernment. You will need to learn to tell the difference between self-servers and servers. With a little education and a general increase in intuition in the next decade, most will no longer fall prey to self-servers. This will lessen their activities on your planet and eventually lead to their withdrawal, since they will no longer find it useful to reincarnate on Earth. Self-servers evolve most quickly on service-to-self planets, where they can best learn the tricks of the trade and experience the negative consequences of their actions.

Earth has always had a service-to-self element. By playing the role of Evil on your planet, self-servers have helped Earth evolve. In personifying your Shadow — the negative within each of you — they are helping you integrate your Shadow.

As Earth moves into fourth density, you will no longer need such a personification. Although the Shadow, or negativity, still exists in fourth density, it will be experienced mostly on internal levels, not acted out. As fourth-density beings, you will still feel drawn to serving yourselves at times, but you will act less frequently on these urges and less harmfully than earlier. In fourth density, you will feel less of a desire to serve yourself, because you will have more of a recognition of who you are serving when you serve others — it is yourself!

The Pleiadians are a peaceful race. They will be your peace ambassadors and teachers. They will show you how a society — indeed, a world — can run smoothly while still honoring its members' differences. This is not an insignificant lesson. Much of the misery on Earth has been caused by one group trying to convince another of its point of view. People on Earth have not yet learned to co-exist with different points of view. That is what you will be learning from the Pleiadians.

Your hierarchical attitudes are part of the problem. You act as if only one way of living and thinking is correct. Your religions are partly responsible for this. Think about how this attitude has affected your relationships. It has reinforced the ego and kept you from loving each other. Now you will learn a new way to structure your perceptions and your societies. This way is non-hierarchical and democratic. This, after all, is what the New Age is about. It is about tolerance, diversity, and equality.

How will you move from hierarchy to equality and cooperation? By changing your belief system. Your society will change as your philosophy changes, which will not be possible except through a change in consciousness. As consciousness changes, so will philosophy and so will your relationships and social structures. A New Age is near — a Golden Age. We are here to see that this transition occurs as smoothly as possible. The Pleiadians will help you form this philosophy. They are experts at creating social systems that allow diversity, tolerance, and equality.

The Pleiadians have always tried to teach you about peace, but you have not been inclined to listen. With the shift in consciousness, this will change. When it does, your world will be revolutionized. Much has been said about a world government by others, much of it controversial. What would a world government mean? Would it mean that Big Brother has come at last? Under your current consciousness, perhaps. However, that is changing. Once enough of you have shifted consciousness, the Pleiadians will help you set up a new world order that is fair, democratic, compassionate, *and* non-hierarchical. This is both possible and, with the Pleiadians' help, probable.

THE SIRIANS

Already quite a bit has been said about the Sirians, since they played such a pivotal role in the human race's early development. They are still involved in your world today. The Sirians are guiding you through your intuition and dreams, through channeling, and through visions. Visions are the most direct way they have been involved with you lately, since they do not materialize or walk among you in physical bodies any longer. There are some reincarnated Sirians among you, but none in materialized bodies.

The Sirians do not have physical bodies, although they can materialize them if they want. As fifth-density beings and beyond, they function beyond matter. This has always been so and one reason they have seemed like gods to you. You saw them materialize and dematerialize before you, something you assumed only a god could do. In addition, many of the forms they took were brilliant, beautiful, and light-filled, making them all the more god-like. Occasionally, they still appear as beautiful light-beings or angels.

Your ancient representations of these light-beings had wings to symbolize their ability to appear, disappear, and move through the air. However, they did not appear to you with wings at first. Only later did they sometimes have wings, in keeping with your image of them. Thus, angels with wings became part of your mythology. But they did not always appear as angels. The form they took depended on who they were appearing to and why.

Although other extraterrestrials also appeared in visions as various characters and as angels, this role fell largely to the Sirians, because they were the ones most involved in the human race's development and evolution. The Sirians acted as teachers and guides more than any other group, although others often helped them. Sirians have been particularly involved in your religious rites and religious societies, including all the mystery schools.

In earlier days, religion was at the center of society. From religion came the ethics that helped societies cohere and function. Laws evolved from these ethics, as did customs, rituals, and traditions. The religious leaders that headed society received guidance directly from the Sirians, so shamans and priests served as bridges between the unseen world of the gods (the Sirians) and the physical world of their own kinsmen. Sometimes these religious leaders were even reincarnated Sirians. Societies have always had members who could communicate with — or channel — these realms, and the Sirians made good use of them. This continues today, of course.

The Sirians described so far were positive, or at least they intended to serve you, even if they sometimes fell short. However, throughout history, there has been another Sirian influence on your planet that has not been so positive. Service-to-self Sirians ("negative" Sirians) have played the role of Satan and Evil on your planet, with the help of some others. Like the positive Sirians, the negative Sirians have materialized and dematerialized as well as reincarnated among you. And through channeling and other psychic means, they have delivered their own version of truth.

Circles of Black Magicians and secret societies with service-to-self intentions formed around these negative Sirians. Then and even now, telling the White Magicians from the Black has not always been easy, since some Black Magicians claim to be White. This should be no surprise. Self-servers have always been willing to do anything to accomplish their goals. That is their credo: "Whatever it takes."

As a result, many unsuspecting and well-meaning people have been used by service-to-self groups without ever realizing it. The leaders of these groups count on drawing in trusting people whom they can manipulate for their own ends. Many of these unsuspecting people never discover they have been deceived.

One reason they are successful is that these circles are sworn to keep their activities secret. Secrecy keeps these circles free of outside influence and interference. They claim secrecy protects the sacred rituals, the same reason White Magicians or mystery schools keep their activities and teachings secret. Unfortunately, while this secrecy protects sacred teachings from getting into the wrong hands, it also protects self-servers who already have their hands on the teachings from being scrutinized.

So, the name of Sirius has been implicated in both White and Black Magic throughout history. The line between the two has sometimes been very thin. This is not because the teachings are not clear about the difference between Black and White Magic, but because the members of the mystery schools and White Magic circles haven't always lived up to the principles of these circles. They have been corrupted by members who have acted like Black Magicians, and by Black Magicians posing as White Magicians to lure people into their circles. The study of esoterica can be treacherous waters.

You are probably wondering what was taught in these secret societies and how this relates to the Sirians. The Sirians founded the mystery schools, which were initially headed and run by Sirians. The mystery schools taught the human race's origin and the origin of the "gods." They also were the means by which new information was introduced to society. Information the Sirians decided was necessary and timely for a society would be given within the mystery schools and then dispensed to appropriate individuals within society.

For instance, if the Sirians decided a civilization could have a certain mathematical formula, it would be introduced either through dreams, channeling, a vision, or other psychic means to someone within the mystery school who had either been trained by the mystery school to receive psychic communication or invited in because of this talent. Then this information would be brought to the attention of others in the mystery school who knew who to relay it to people outside of the mystery school.

So, you could think of mystery schools as the "think tanks" of bygone days. They came up with the ideas that propelled society to new levels scientifically, mathematically, linguistically, architecturally, agriculturally, and in every conceivable way. The mystery schools served, like shamans and priests, as a bridge between the seen and unseen worlds.

The Sirians created one set of religious teachings for mystery school initiates and another for the rest of the population. So, two distinct forms of religion developed: the esoteric and the exoteric. These two forms were necessary, as the Sirians saw it, to accommodate vastly different levels of understanding. Most of the people on Earth then were at a primitive stage in their evolution, while a few were evolved way beyond them.

Those who were more evolved were primarily Sirians and others reincarnated to guide humanity: Star People and Walk-ins. These were the "gods" incarnate, or at the very least their helpers. In the mystery schools, they were taught about their origins and their mission, and shown how to regain and further develop their psychic abilities. Everyone in the mystery schools was potentially psychic, but not everyone was developed. Consequently, the mystery schools came to be known as a place where the psychic arts were taught.

While this was going on inside the mystery schools, those outside were being taught a religious system designed for them by the Sirians to serve the Sirians' goals. For instance, the Sirians needed to instill in people the importance of obedience, since the Sirians' effectiveness depended on people's willingness to follow their teachings. So, they created a hierarchical model of the universe headed by an authoritarian God: Jehovah. Jehovah was only one form of this imperious god. Every religion established in every culture in your early history had its version of Jehovah. By setting up a hierarchy with an authoritarian god at its head and religious leaders as representatives of this god, the Sirians were able to maintain control of the people. The Sirians could shape what people believed by having these priests, who were trained in the mystery schools, tell people what to believe. This meant they also shaped society, since society developed from the ideas and principles handed down by the priests.

From time to time, negative Sirians took on the role of priest and hierophant and sought power over people for their own purposes, rather than for the good of society. Societies headed by negative Sirians eventually fell, because they became infested with corruption, vice, and licentiousness. Societies headed by negative Sirians could not cohere for long, because they lacked the principles that bind a society. So, despite some tyranny by the positive Sirians, they did at least provide people with principles on which a society could be built. Without imposing such principles, these early societies would have fallen to their own greed and corruption, just like the negative Sirian societies.

Another feature of the exoteric religions the Sirians established was adherence to tradition. This helped the Sirians maintain their authority and control the rate of change within society. By teaching people to value tradition and their elders, they established a set of fundamental beliefs. Without this, what they were teaching might not have carried over from one generation to the next. Rituals were created to contain these teachings in a form that could be passed down from one generation to the next. Such a vehicle for transmitting knowledge was particularly necessary in preliterate times.

Rituals were also a way of opening people up to the Absolute by altering consciousness. Imbedded in the rituals were ways of altering consciousness and loosening the ego's hold, so that some degree of transcendence could be experienced. Once people had moved beyond their egos in ritual, convincing them of the value of the universal principles imparted by the priests was easy. In these states, they experienced the beauty and wisdom of the priests' teachings, something that was not so obvious while in their ego-consciousness. So, rituals reinforced the teachings being given to the people by the priests. Unfortunately, the negative Sirians also found a way to use ritual for their ends.

So, the Sirian priests gave the people spiritual truths in a form that would be accepted by them and which would continue to relegate power to themselves. This was for the good of the people. The negative Sirians, on the other hand, had different intentions: they wanted to enslave people. In making the people dependent on the priests, the positive Sirians had left them open to manipulation by the Dark Brotherhood, who from time to time managed to infiltrate the priesthood.

The Sirian priests were aware of the negative Sirians' manipulations. However, they could only stop them after they had committed blatant offenses. Therefore, many negative Sirians still managed to perpetrate their negativity, fear, and confusion surreptitiously. Negative Sirians worked insidiously within the priest system and even infiltrated some mystery schools. The priests viewed the negative element as a normal part of living in a world of polarities. They accepted the negative Sirians' presence and allowed them to operate, except when they openly broke the rules. This is how it is today, too.

As a result of this infiltration, some teachings became corrupted and many were used for ill. What remains today of the teachings are fragments mixed with distortions, although the general teachings can be pieced together. Many of the teachings given to you by the Sirians can be found in your occult literature, along with the distortions. Many of them dealt with the development of psychic abilities.

Both Black and White Magicians develop and use psychic powers, but for different reasons. These special abilities would make them formidable opponents, but White Magicians do not engage in battle with Black

Magicians. Black Magicians do, however, try to undermine the good works of White Magicians. In fact, much of their energy goes into this. Black Magicians manage to succeed in many of their endeavors, since White Magicians are sworn to use their powers only to serve, not to stop negativity in the world. Negativity is not necessarily a problem in a universe that evolves through the interplay of polarities. Negativity is a fact of life and serves a purpose. Only when negativity overwhelms the positive does it become a problem.

The world's condition is one of increasing polarization. As the forces for Good have become stronger, so have the forces for Evil. Both positive and negative Star People and Walk-ins have emerged in greater numbers on your planet of late. Perhaps you thought Star People and Walk-ins could only be positive, since they are more evolved than the average human being. This is not true. Star People and Walk-ins from fourth- and fifth-density service-to-self planets have arrived on your planet as well. They are as interested in taking advantage of you as the others are in helping you. As a result, there are many more Star People and Walk-ins on your planet now than ever before, all coming to help or hinder during this critical period.

The negative Star People and Walk-ins are primarily negative Sirians and negative Orions. They are here for the same purpose, although they have no intention of sharing the spoils if they succeed. So, although they are cooperating now, they would quarrel over anything they managed to obtain. They are the cult leaders and those drawn to the Dark Arts and Satanism. They are the Jim Joneses and Reverend Moons of the world.

They are easily spotted: They are charismatic, intelligent, revolutionary, unconventional, and skilled in leadership and communication. They have what it takes to deceive and manipulate naïve, idealistic youth and other vulnerable people. Some are in it for the power, while others are trying to undermine the Earth's transformation. Many of the latter are not even conscious of this mission, but are acting on unconscious suggestions received through dreams and intuition. However, others are eminently conscious of the plan, usually through psychic means like channeling. So, just as positive extraterrestrials are working through Star People and Walk-ins, so are negative extraterrestrials.

Psychic abilities are therefore very important to both the negative plan and the positive one. Psychic abilities are being used by both the positive and the negative forces to accomplish their goals. This is one reason for increased interest in them. Both positive and negative Star People and Walk-ins are clambering to develop these abilities. Some are conscious of why they want them, but most are not. Information about how to develop psychic abilities is being made available now by both groups.

The negative extraterrestrials' plan is loose. Negative Star People and Walk-ins are to do whatever they can to confuse people, instill fear, undermine positive action, and foster distrust of the government. The methods are not prescribed but up to the individual. Most of these negative Star People and Walk-ins are full of anger, pessimism, and other forms of negativity. Many do not understand the motivation behind their negative actions but feel compelled to act out their negativity. As a result, they attract others who are equally out of harmony. They aren't in harmony with them either, but that doesn't matter. They are more comfortable around other negative people than positive people.

Negative Star People and Walk-ins who are aware of their mission are as dedicated to it as positive Star People and Walk-ins are to theirs. However, they are less power-ful than the servers, because they are less evolved than them in nearly every way, even though they are still far more intellectually evolved than the average human being. They do have cleverness and intellect on their side, but that is not enough to make them a match for positive forces.

Yes, negative forces also have psychic powers. But with-out the ability to organize and cooperate, psychic powers are not as useful as you might think. Not being able to cooperate and subordinate themselves is the negatives' worst handicap. This flaw greatly diminishes their power. Even though they have roles, they often do not fulfill them, because they are too busy fighting over autonomy and leadership. They all want to lead and resent taking direc-tions, even when it is in their best interest. Because of this, the negatives are not a serious threat. If they were, the positive forces would find a way to render them ineffective. But they will allow some negativity to exist in this free-will world of yours.

The Sirius star system is unique in having one of the largest numbers of fifth-density self-servers anywhere. Since they are in your corner of the universe, that is significant. They are part of your galactic family, so you reincarnate there and they reincarnate here. All the extraterrestrials being introduced to you through these pages are mem-bers of your galactic family. This means that when you die, you might not come back to Earth immediately but reincarnate on any of the other planets in your galactic family of a similar density. There you may stay only briefly or for many incarnations before you reincarnate some-where else. You may be used to thinking of yourself as reincarnating only on one planet (Earth) repeatedly until you evolve beyond the physical plane. However, you actually reincarnate on other planets besides Earth while you are evolving through the physical plane (third and fourth density).

You are considered a Star Person on the planet you go to only if you have evolved beyond the density of that planet. For instance, if you are third density and you reincarnate on a third-density planet, you would not be considered a Star Person. But if you are fourth density and you reincarnate on a third-density planet, you would. The difference between Star People and others is that Star People do not reincarnate on a planet for their own growth (although they do evolve there), as much as to help that world.

There are third-, fourth-, fifth-, sixth-, and seventh-density planets in your galactic family. So Star People and Walk-ins visiting Earth may be fourth-, fifth-, sixth-, or seventh-density. Seventh-density Star People are extremely rare. Christ was sixth-density. Fifth-density Star People are fairly common, as are fourth-density. Fourth-density Star People are a little more advanced than the ordinary Earth inhabitant, similar to the old souls on your planet.

To add to the confusion, time is not actually linear: past, present, and future coexist simultaneously. This means that you could meet extraterrestrials from the past and from the future, not just from the present. As you might expect, extraterrestrials from the past are less evolved than their present or future selves. The negative Orions, for instance, are from the past, while the positive Orions are from the present. The negative Sirians, on the other hand, are from the present. This is the major difference between the negative Orions and the negative Sirians. The negative Sirians are more advanced than the negative Orions.

We are leading up to the next chapter, about the Orions, by way of describing the Sirians, because the Orions and the Sirians are closely related. The Orions existed within the Sirius star system before they moved to the Orion star system. The negative Orions enter your world the same way the Sirians do: through reincarnation, Walk-in, and materialization. Unlike the Sirians of late, the negative Orions have been materializing on your planet recently, most commonly as the infamous Men in Black. We will say more about them in the next chapter.

Because the negative Sirians are more evolved than the negative Orions, they often act as guides to them. That is one of their roles. They are the ones sending messages to the negative Orion Star People and Walk-ins, psychically and through the subconscious mind. Other negative Orions are working with them, but the negative Sirians are heading this operation. The negative Sirians figure they will use the negative Orions and then get rid of them. The negative Orions are aware of this, but they are not intimidated by it. A sense of invincibility is another failing of self-servers.

The positive Sirians are not concerned about the negative Sirians' activities on your planet. They understand their methods and are following their activities closely. This is one advantage the positives have over the negatives: they understand the psychology of self-servers, while the opposite is not true. The positive Sirians will let the negative Sirians go about their business until the negatives interfere with them. When this happens, the positive Sirians will stop the negative Sirians.

Your planet is a battleground of sorts, but that shouldn't surprise you. Throughout history, many have seen it as a battleground for Good and Evil. This is truer now than ever. Fortunately, the forces for Good still far outweigh the forces for Evil, even though more of each exist than ever before. Moreover, Good has always had advantages over Evil.

The positive Sirians will continue to work through channels, psychics, the subconscious mind, and dreams. They may manifest briefly if necessary, but mostly they will remain hidden. This in no way diminishes their importance. They have always been the most significant group of extraterrestrials involved with your world. They will continue to guide and serve you during these times, and they will do it with more understanding and wisdom than ever before because of what they have learned from being your teachers and your "gods."

THE ORIONS

The negative Orions like to think they are important to the negatives' mission to capture the Earth, but their importance and impact are minor. Hence, the brevity of this chapter. The negative Orions are the most visible of the service-to-self extraterrestrials, usually taking the form of Men in Black. Others have arrived as Star People and Walk-ins. Thus, the negative Orions are involved with Earth in all the ways already described: through materialization as Men in Black, as Star People and Walk-ins, and through channeling and other psychic means.

Since negative Orions are third-, fourth-, and fifth-density, not every Orion who reincarnates here would be considered a Star Person. Third-density Orions would not. Most of the negative Orions on your planet are reincarnations and fourth-density Star People and Walk-ins, making the Orions as a whole the least evolved of the extraterrestrial groups visiting you. Men in Black, who are fifth-density, are rare, although quite visible.

Men in Black are fifth-density service-to-self Orions who temporarily take on a body (through materialization) to achieve their negative goals. Thus, they can affect matter when they need to, and dematerialize it when it is no longer expedient. The bodies they take on are usually of male gender, dressed anachronistically in a 1940s style dark suit and hat. They look pale, sickly, unattractive, and emotionless. They impress people as extremely odd, not only because of their clothing and lack of emotion, but because of their whole demeanor. They have not studied your culture sufficiently to imitate you well, so they seem strange to you.

The Men in Black are aware that they seem strange to you. That's fine with them, as they are not here to win your favor or even to fool you, but to go about their business. Your reactions rarely interfere with this, so they have not bothered to refine their act. In fact, they like startling and scaring people. After all, this is something self-servers enjoy, so they are not the least bit concerned about what you think of them. The more mystery and fear they can create, the better. However, mostly, they are just trying to get their work done.

The Men in Black are following a plan. They want you to believe that anyone who claims to have seen a UFO is being spied on by your government. Consequently, they pose as government agents and threaten those who make such claims. They are not trying to cover up evidence of UFOs; they just want you to think your government will do anything to keep this information secret. It's not hard to leave people with this impression, since your government has, indeed, been running a UFO cover-up. That is what makes the Men in Black's job so easy. The Men in Black are drawing attention to the government's cover-up by acting so strangely and by threatening people.

The reason they want you to think your government is intimidating people is that they want you to believe your government is a threat to its citizens. They don't want you to believe in your government — or in democracy, for that matter. Democracy is counter to any political system they would ever create, since they believe in subjugating people — which is what they hope to do to you.

These Orions come from a system (in the past) with only two social roles: rulers and slaves. They believe they have the right and the duty to subjugate people and that those who succeed deserve to rule. They also believe that those who don't succeed deserve to be slaves. Slaves in the Orion system also believe this, for this philosophy has pervaded their thinking for generations. So the oppressed have internalized their oppression so fully that the rulers have to do very little to keep them serving them. This leaves two classes of people: perpetrators and victims.

These Orions have reincarnated on Earth throughout history as either perpetrators or victims. On Earth, they act out one or the other of these roles until they learn to act differently.

Victims are easy to spot, since they are victimized repeatedly by a variety of people in a variety of ways. They keep playing this role until they decide they won't take it anymore. At this point, they often become crusaders for victims' rights, which is the jewel in this experience and the balancing of it.

Perpetrators also remain perpetrators until it no longer works for them. Their reformation usually occurs through role reversal by being victimized, enslaved, or incarcerated.

The roles of perpetrator and victim are not easily balanced on Orion, where the ideology supports them. This is one reason they reincarnate on Earth and elsewhere where victimization is not tolerated. You are not as lost to negativity as you think! Even though much victimization occurs on Earth, your religious beliefs do not support it. Your religions are founded on positive values, even if people sometimes fail to live up to them.

So you see, the Earth is a place where polarities can be balanced. While Orions are balancing their polarities by reincarnating here, they are providing the Earth with some of the negativity it needs to evolve. So a symbiotic relationship has always existed between the Orion system and Earth: you need them and they need you. It may seem like an odd way to need someone, but the negative pole or service-to-self is not viewed by the Creator as evil. The terms "good" and "evil" have been used for your sake, since you can relate to them. But the Creator's view is that all creations are good.

The Men in Black have a few other tasks besides undermining people's trust in the government. One is to collect information for the negative extraterrestrials. They do this by traveling about and observing the activities of people and, on occasion, interacting with them. They sometimes stay for days on Earth going about such business, making it necessary for them to eat, sleep, and travel by ordinary means. They do not travel by dematerializing for short trips, because it takes too much energy. Sometimes they hitchhike, since this is one way they can get from place to place without currency. When they need currency, they either materialize it (which takes considerable knowledge of currency) or they steal it, primarily by dematerializing it and re-materializing it.

The Men in Black often get the information they want from people because people are so stunned by them that they just give it to them. People are particularly unlikely to be rude to exceptional-looking people, and the Men in Black certainly are that. So, despite the fear and suspicion they evoke, they easily get what they want from surprised and unsuspecting people. Usually what they are after is information about people: who lives where and with whom. In asking such questions, they are trying to find those whom they have heard might be useful to them.

They are not very clever at tracking people down. It often takes them many visits to Earth just to find one of the people they are looking for, since they are so unfamiliar with your ways. Usually, they are looking for Orion Star People and Walk-ins to inform them of their identity and the negatives' mission. However, they are often unsuccessful, because if the individual is not already aware of being a Star Person or Walk-in, the Men in Black are not very well received. Thus, the Orions are bunglers, who take their work seriously but whom others do not take very seriously — including the other extraterrestrials!

Positive Orions have now joined the scene. They have only recently become involved with Earth, primarily by working through channels and psychics. They also are acting as guides to their negative comrades, but with little effect. The negative Orions are more open to the negative Sirians.

The positive Orions evolved from the negative Orions after some very dark times in the Orion system. During the darkest of times, a savior — an avatar — was born to them, who changed their service-to-self beliefs. As a result, the Orions evolved from service-to-self to service-to-others, but only after many thousands of years. The positive Orions are contacting you from the Orion present, while the negative Orions are from their past. They regret the negative Orions' behavior, although they also understand that someone must play the part of negativity on your planet. They ardently hope to serve you.

THE ZETA RETICULI

The history of this race is not only interesting but it is also important to you. It is important because you are traveling down the road they traveled many millennia ago. They regret that they traveled this road and have much to teach you about where they went wrong and what they would have done differently. You are giving them the chance to redo their past by providing them with the genetic keys to go backwards in time. You also are giving them the opportunity to balance their mistakes by teaching you. This is your relationship with the Zeta Reticuli.

The Zetas only recently became aware of you. They had never interacted with the human race before their arrival in mid-century. They heard the call for help sent out by your extraterrestrial guardians at the advent of the atomic age. When civilizations reach this point in their development (and many inevitably do), warnings are sent out to those who might be affected. The Zetas received this call, because it was thought they might be able to convince you to turn away from nuclear power. The Elders of your planet, the Sirians in particular, saw the possibility of mutual aid and told the Zetas about you.

The Zetas were elated to discover there was a race so like them genetically and one to which they could pay their karmic dues. They eagerly accepted the challenge of helping you and, in the process, of helping themselves. The only problem was that approaching you directly would probably create too much disturbance on Earth. This had to be handled carefully. So the extraterrestrials guarding your planet devised a plan.

Their plan was to introduce themselves gradually to you, to secure soul-agreements with certain people to help, and to save genetic material in case you destroyed yourselves and your environment with nuclear weapons before they could stop you. They also planned to use the Pleiadians as go-betweens and peacemakers. Starting in the late 1940s, the Zetas began observing you and abducting people for their genetic and experimental needs. They abducted only those from whom they received permission on a soul level. And, for their protection, they arranged for abductees to forget the abduction. Nevertheless, some still recalled these events through hypnosis. This was one of the plan's imperfections. The Zetas did not mean to traumatize their subjects. They regret the problems this has caused people, but they feel justified (based on the soul-agreements) in continuing their activities. On the positive side, the accounts of abductees have helped the public gradually become acquainted with extraterrestrials.

The Zetas carry out their work mostly at night, when they are least likely to be perceived and when their subjects are likely to be asleep. They appear in the daytime only in remote, isolated areas where they will not be observed by bystanders. They enter people's homes by disassembling and reassembling their atoms, rather than by going through doors or windows. They can do the same for abductees, who either travel with them physically or in their astral body. Sometimes the Zetas find it easier to just use the astral body, while leaving the physical body behind in a state of protected sleep. But when they need the physical body, they propel it through walls and through the air to their spaceship, where the necessary medical equipment is waiting.

This can be done so quietly and with so little intrusion that others in the house are unaware of what is happening. Zetas also can make themselves invisible, but they prefer not to use their energy this way unless they have to. They are skilled in hypnosis as well, which enables them to put household members or other possible spectators into deep states, from which they will not awaken until a certain signal is given.

You may be wondering why the Zetas don't use the Pleiadians for the abductions if they are so concerned about frightening people. They don't use Pleiadians because the Pleiadians do not have the technical skills needed to transport people, and because most people don't recall the night's activities anyway. Besides, abduction even by kindly, human-looking beings would be disturbing to most people. In the end, only a small percentage of abductees recall their abductions, which gives you an idea of how common they are. They are a nightly affair.

The Zeta abductions are different from the Greys' in several ways. First, although both the Zetas and the Greys are using your genes to improve their species, their intentions are very different. The Zetas intend to return to their home bases and resume their lives once they have regained their health and viability. The Greys, on the other hand, hope to remain on Earth with you as their slaves. That is quite a difference.

Second, while the Zetas return their subjects unharmed, the Greys have been known to kill, mutilate, and dismember their subjects, as you might do in your laboratory experiments with animals. Many missing persons, including many children, have been taken by the Greys and killed, although painlessly. The Greys have no more respect for human life than most of you have for animals or plants. They view you as a lower form of life, even though you could be their ancestors. You are to them what cave men or apes might be to you: a scientific curiosity. This should cause you to reflect on your treatment of other forms of life!

The third difference is that the Greys purposely incite fear in their subjects, because they are studying fear in human beings. Once they find a way to create a permanent state of fear in you, they can control you. Since fear is caused by chemicals, their plan is feasible and clever, befitting the most diabolical of self-servers.

The Zetas, on the other hand, do not want to frighten you, although they realize they do. The Zetas try to communicate safety and calmness to you. However, not everyone receives their soothing telepathic messages, because they are often blocked by fright. They don't know how to communicate with you except telepathically, so they are at a loss when you can't "hear" them. When this happens, they take special care to erase the memory of the frightening event. But as we have said, they are not always successful in this.

Another major difference between the Zetas and the Greys is that the Greys lie to you, and the Zetas don't. The Zetas communicate little rather than lie to you. When they choose not to communicate with you, it is for your own good. The Greys, on the other hand, lie and confuse people. Lies are an essential part of their plan.

So, how can you tell the Greys from the Zetas when they look so much alike? You can tell by how you feel. Granted, even an encounter with a Zeta can be frightening. Still, beneath the fright will be a sense of serenity or trust, which will not be present around the Greys. Around them, you feel frightened to death — and rightly so! The trick is not to feel frightened around either of them. Not being frightened will help the Zetas' work and obstruct the Greys', making it less likely the Greys will harm you. Hopefully, knowing this will help you overcome your fear.

The good news is that most abductions are by Zetas, since there are fewer Greys. Furthermore, only a small percentage of abductions by Greys result in disappearance and death. This may be of little comfort to the hundreds who have lost children to the Greys over the last forty years. The Greys take children because they are easy to snatch and keep in a state of fright. The Greys also are responsible for the cattle mutilations, which are part of their scientific investigations.

The Greys are cowards in many respects and have neither the Zetas' cleverness nor their technical know-how. This explains why their spacecraft are the ones found crashed. Their actions are despicable and must be stopped. However, as long as the public remains in the dark about who is responsible for the cattle mutilations and missing persons, little can be done to stop them.

Their activities will not be allowed to continue for long. Soon the positive extraterrestrials will announce themselves, denounce the Greys, and help you rid yourselves of them. The Zetas will be especially useful to you in expelling the Greys. The irony is that the Zetas look like the Greys and are therefore unlikely to be trusted by you. You will have to trust someone in the times ahead, though, since you do not have the technology or understanding to face the negative extraterrestrial threat by yourselves.

For over forty years, your government's experience with extraterrestrials has been negative and threatening. Your government and others have yet to establish relations with a positive extraterrestrial. This is because the positives have not made themselves available to your government, nor will they for a while. They have a specific plan, and they are not ready to come forward yet. Let's look at what we can of this plan.

The positive extraterrestrials are not interfering with the negatives' interactions with your government, because they believe it is best not to get involved yet. The positives will intervene when you are finally ready to admit that extraterrestrials exist. This point has not arrived yet. Those within your government in charge of the extraterrestrial threat are still too afraid to tell the people what is going on.

They are afraid because of the negatives' threats and because they believe it is their duty to handle the situation without arousing the public's fear. They also are afraid of what this knowledge would do to the world's economies and the global situation. There are many reasons for their remaining silent all these years. They have been hoping to contain this problem and end the threat without people ever finding out. This is not realistic, but understandable.

However, in keeping silent, they have gotten in deeper with the negative extraterrestrials, whom they now realize they can neither control nor defeat. When your government becomes genuinely concerned, the positives will step in and offer their aid. The sight of attractive, human-looking extraterrestrials will be most welcome and inspiring of trust, if they can convince your government of their identity and their good intentions.

Only after relations and trust have been established between the Pleiadians and your government will the rest of the story be introduced, including the Zetas themselves. At that time, you will be taught to distinguish the Zetas from the Greys. You also will be taught how to handle the Greys and given means of protecting yourselves from them. The negatives' plot will be exposed, and they will have no more power over you. With the Zetas' help, divesting the Greys of their power will not be difficult.

The Zetas understand the Greys like no one else, since they come from the same planet and genetic stock. The Zetas know the Greys' physical and psychological weaknesses, they understand their technology, and they know how to overpower every one of their tactics. The Zetas are your best allies against the Greys. The Zetas will help you, out of appreciation for your race and out of karmic duty.

Over the last forty years, the Zetas have become very involved with you emotionally, if you could use that word. They see you as a valiant and energetic race, one full of potential and promise, given the proper guidance. They believe you can make the changes within yourselves necessary to sustain human life on Earth for many more millennia.

In the meantime, the Zetas are trying to preserve your species, as well as your plants and animals, in case you take the road they did. They, too, received visitors to their planet who tried to convince them to settle their differences peacefully, but they did not listen. They were sure the solution was ridding themselves of a group they considered evil. The war they had was a war of Good versus Evil, or service-to-others versus service-to-self. The servers felt justified in doing anything to eradicate the evil on their planet — even using nuclear weapons. This was a holy war with nuclear weapons and a distortion of the service path. Had your planet had these weapons during the Crusades, you might have followed a similar course then.

Their planet was so divided between these two factions that negotiation was impossible. The standoff was similar to the Arab/Israeli standoff today, where — without compromise — the likelihood is mutual annihilation. The Zeta's experience showed that one's beliefs, even righteous ones — or *especially* righteous ones — can be dangerous. No moral value, or supposed moral value, is worth destroying life over. Some of you realize this; the Zetas all realize this now.

The history of the Zetas is lengthy, since their stay underground lasted thousands of years. One doesn't evolve from being human-looking to looking like the "creatures" the Zetas and Greys are now overnight, even with genetic engineering. The same is true for returning to their prior state: it will take the Zetas millennia to regain their ability to feel emotions, to reproduce, and to process food as you do. However, thousands of years is a mere in-breath in the lifetime of a species.

These two factions went underground with their differences intact. The conflict could not continue underground, however, because they were separated by rock. As a result, the two factions developed differently. The service-to-others group learned from their mistake and vowed never to use violence to overcome evil again. Ironically, by indulging themselves in the ultimate destruction — the destruction of their beloved planet — they had learned to respect life. The service-to-self group developed into a service-to-self society (the Greys) that continued to fight among themselves. They didn't learn to respect life, but power.

The lesson the Zetas learned is a major one in every humanoid race's development. They now understand that only when their lives are threatened should offensive measures be taken, and this out of respect for their own lives. If offensive measures are not employed for self-preservation, a society may become dominated by self-servers and maintained by servants, as happened in the Orion system. Rarely have people on Earth held to such a guideline. Most have either chosen offensive strategies or martyrdom, without giving due consideration to the middle path of peaceful protest and self-protection. Your nations have glorified warriors and your religions have glorified martyrs.

The Zeta servers would not have had to destroy their planet to protect their lives or uphold their freedom, although many believed they had no choice. The self-servers, as in most societies, were simply not that powerful. The self-servers led the servers to believe they had no recourse but to use their nuclear weapons. This use of deception and fear is part of service-to-self tactics everywhere. The servers believed they had no recourse, because the self-servers convinced them of this. Therefore, the self-servers saw themselves as victors. They had succeeded in creating such fear that people had annihilated life on their own planet. What a victory!

You probably find it hard to follow this logic, and understandably so. You have to understand that self-servers do not see things globally. They don't see the larger picture, only their immediate goals. This is why they are dying now. Such a society can exist only so long before it collapses in on itself. They still do not consider their predicament a defeat, however. They will not admit defeat until they have completely died off.

The Greys are a dying race, and soon will no longer serve as vehicles for service-to-self. Many Greys will change paths as a result of their extinction, never to return to service-to-self again. This is the natural course of service-to-self. All self-servers eventually become servers, and often only after a similar course. The positives understand this and are willing to let the Greys play this out to the finish their own way, so that the greatest number of Greys will learn the futility of their path. This is a spiritual turning point for them.

The Zetas may be your closest allies, because no one else has as much motivation for being involved with you now as they do. The other positive extraterrestrials have been involved with you throughout your history. Only the Zetas have recently come to your aid, and only they have a fate that is so intimately tied to yours and yours to them. You have spiritual, biological, and emotional lessons to learn from each other. The Zetas have much to offer you in exchange for your trust and your help.

They want you to trust them, because they know they can help you. They also want you to trust them because they need you. Trust, however, will be a big issue, thanks to the Greys' misadventures with your government. The Pleiadians' tasks will be to help you learn to trust the Zetas. The Sirians will orchestrate the plan but remain invisible. So the Pleiadians and the Zetas will be the most visible of those involved with you; however, many others from all over will be helping in their own way.

To prepare the Zetas for their future and for their meeting with you, the Pleiadians are teaching them about emotions. The Zetas realize that, because they do not understand your emotions, they don't handle you as well as they might during your encounters. They are baffled by your fright, your extremes in expression, and your openness. They don't know what to make of such expressiveness, since they themselves have nothing to express but information. They have no capability for intimacy and sharing as a result. In short, they have no capacity for personal relationship.

This is a characteristic of the Zetas that will be baffling to you. They do cooperate and they do love, yet they are impersonal and uncommitted in how they love. They have no families, and consequently no sense of belonging with particular individuals, only to their race. This has its advantages in building a society, as they view each other as equals and as equally valuable. Their race is ideal in this respect.

However, without physical differences and emotions, the Zeta lifestyle is predictable and dull, and spiritual evolution doesn't proceed as rapidly as it might. Evolution on the physical plane occurs through the interplay of polarities, of which the emotions (i.e. love/hate and happiness/ sadness) are a part. The Zetas do have their conflicts. But they are about processes and procedures, not needs and attitudes. Thus, their race has become robotized because of their lack of emotions.

Maybe this helps you appreciate your emotions. The goal of your Earthly lifetimes is not to rid yourselves of your emotions. The goal is to use your emotional experiences to evolve beyond being ruled by them. As you move into fourth density, you will still have some fear, anger, guilt, and sadness, but you will not act on these emotions as you do now. Your relationship to your emotions will change, not the emotions themselves.

This is the step the Zetas never learned to make. They never learned to have their emotions without being ruled by them. Instead, they chose to rid themselves of them through genetic engineering. This hindered their evolution, especially their ability to experience unconditional love, for the evolution of emotions is the evolution of unconditional love. We have said that the Zetas experience love, and they do. However, their love is impersonal. It is different from the love you will evolve in the course of your evolution, and different from the love they would have evolved had they retained their emotions.

The Zetas have so much to learn from you about emotions and, consequently, about love. This may sound strange, knowing they are many thousands of years more evolved than you intellectually and technologically. However, their evolution has been arrested emotionally. Now they must go back and catch up, if they are to survive into the future.

They have the greatest admiration for your courage in struggling with the emotions they chose to eliminate. They may not understand emotions, but they know their importance now. And they know that your unfathomable emotions hold the key to their future. They respect you because you have something they so desperately want and need, and they want to help you for the same reason. However, their love for you goes beyond what they want and need. They love you because they see themselves in you and, like looking into the mirror of their past, they are mystified and astonished at the reflection they see.

THE GREYS

The Greys have been creating problems for your government ever since their first downed craft was discovered in the New Mexico desert in 1947. The creatures you found (for that is what you considered them) both horrified and mystified you. The authorities were immediately notified and the few civilians present were ordered to be silent. The Air Force whisked away the remains of the fallen craft and its inhabitants, one of which was still alive. A special task force was organized to examine the findings and give recommendations. The one surviving extraterrestrial was taken to a laboratory and kept under strict supervision day and night, where after some years it succumbed to an unknown illness. This was your first encounter with the Greys.

Other governments have had some encounters with the Greys, but none so far-reaching or complex as yours. The United States is the only government that has had ongoing communication with the Greys, including a treaty, which has turned out to be a sham. Other governments have merely encountered the Greys and other extraterrestrials briefly, and kept reports on these meetings and other sightings.

The Greys are more interested in the United States than in other countries, because it sees the United States as the most powerful nation. They are right about that, but they have underestimated your intelligence and your love for freedom. If it were not for their advanced technology, you would be a formidable foe. Their technology is not nearly as powerful as they would like you to think, however.

Your government doesn't know what to do about the Greys. It has had relations with them for over forty years, during which time several administrations have come and gone. Each administration during those years has known something about the Greys, the treaty with them, and the history of your relationship with them. However, over the years, continuity has been lost, facts have been confused, and now no one knows the entire story. This, along with the Greys' lies, has made this situation less and less manageable over the years. The ones in charge of this no longer know what the truth is, since none of them were around for the initial recoveries and treaty. What has happened is a little like "Pass the Secret," where, in the end, no one knows what the secret was.

This is fine with the Greys. The longer they can keep their activities secret and keep you in a state of confusion and division, the better. They are trying to back your government into a corner so that it will do something drastic, like detonate a nuclear device. By locating in the United States, they hope that you will destroy your country while trying to protect yourselves from them. They don't want the government to tell the public about them, because they believe they can incite those heading this secret operation to attack them.

The Greys believe the likelihood of you destroying your-selves is less if the public knows about them. They know many people are communicating with the positive extra-terrestrials, whom they realize are their real challenge. The Greys don't want you to have any information about them that would foil their plan, and there are plenty of people who could expose the Greys and their deceptions — if people believed them. The Greys realize that time is limited before the positives come forward and expose them. They only hope they can create so much confusion before then that no one will listen to the positives when this does hap-pen. That is their hope. However, they are not taking something into account — something that will win your trust, something we cannot tell you about yet.

The Greys have allies helping them, primarily the negative Orions and their Men in Black. These two groups have been communicating with each other and support-ing each other's moves throughout these forty years. However, they have only been cooperating because it has been expedient. If that changes, they will begin fighting with each other. This has already happened several times during their so-called alliance, with a few casualties on each side. They are not opposed to killing each other if they think someone among them is interfering with their goals.

The Greys and the Orions are a mismatch. They work awkwardly together, because they come from very differ-ent cultures. The Orions try to dominate everyone, which has caused considerable problems in working as a unit. On the other hand, the Greys are used to functioning as one body. Because of these cultural differences, the Greys see the Orions as disorganized and unreliable, while the Orions see the Greys as easily manipulated sheep. However, the Greys have their own brand of leadership. It is leadership by the whole, in their own unique, mystifying way. Operating in unison as they do is a contradiction in terms for service-to-self, but they do it.

Because of their differences, the Greys and the Orions are not getting along well on this mission. The dissension among them is rendering their operation ineffective. Neither has even tried to understand each other or to make use of the other's good qualities. Ironically, the Greys and the Orions don't see themselves as ineffectual nor do they recognize their insufficiencies. This makes them all the more vulnerable to failure.

The Greys also are vulnerable physically. Greys who have been on Earth for any length of time have had their life spans drastically reduced, and some have already died as a result. The others, who are circling the Earth in space-craft, number only in the thousands, not the tens of thousands. How they think they can enslave you with so few and so little ability to sustain themselves on Earth is a wonder. This can only be explained by the nature of service-to-self, which is egocentric, naïve, and lacking in a sense of personal vulnerability. The Greys' behavior can only be understood when you realize they are psychologically like children.

Like children, they are incapable of seeing life from someone else's perspective. More advanced beings understand this and don't expect them to operate other-wise, just as you would not expect a child to act like an adult. More advanced beings don't feel at odds with self-servers. They understand this level of development and want to help them. We mention this so that you can begin to see them for what they are, not for what they think they are. They are not a serious threat to you.

Self-servers can only enslave those inclined toward victimization. Certainly some in your population are so inclined, but humanity as a whole is not. Your country in particular honors independence, freedom, fairness, and equality — all values abhorrent to service-to-self. So the United States is the least likely to fall to service-to-self aggressors, yet, it is the one with whom they have established relations.

They have only gotten as far as they have because they have been playing on your fear and your belief in violence as a solution to problems. They are mirroring your own aggressiveness and frightening you with it. Their tactics are not actually like yours: they do not conquer with weapons. They are pretending they do, because they know this is what you are afraid of and what you expect from an enemy. They are playing your game and scaring you with it. Their game, however, is more subtle and insidious. They are playing that game, too.

They conquer through fear: they dominate others by arousing their fears. Therefore, they study what causes fear within a race and then use that against them. They understand that fear is the real weapon. You learned that, too, during the recent Cold War. What you may not have realized is that you could have won the Cold War even if the opposition had only believed you had those weapons. Neither side had any way of knowing for certain what weapons the other had or how many, so deception would have worked as well as stockpiling weapons. At least deception would not have drained your economy, which has become a liability for you. The Greys are not unintelligent, even if they are egocentric!

As we have said, the Greys are studying how fear is produced biochemically in human beings. They also are studying what makes you afraid. They have figured this out now and are nearly ready to carry out their plan. They will not be given an opportunity to, however. The positives will allow them to go only so far. Too much is at stake to let them continue beyond a certain point. Be assured that the positive extraterrestrials know exactly what the Greys are up to and how to handle them.

The negatives believe the positives are weak: they see their noninterference as weakness and a license. They don't understand the positives' reasons for noninterference nor do they know how powerful they are, because the positives have never opposed them. They haven't needed to. This has led the negatives to conclude that the positives will not oppose them now. They are wrong.

Earth and its people are much too precious to lose. Despite the vastness of the universe, the Earth plays an important role in the universe. In its uniqueness, it is important to the whole. It provides an experience for those living on it that could not be duplicated anywhere else.

The negatives alone are not powerful enough to overtake the Earth. However, the Earth is vulnerable now, and the concern is that they could conquer you by throwing off your transition or inciting you to destroy yourselves with nuclear weapons. Only in that sense are the Greys dangerous.

They know this, too. They know you are vulnerable and that they have an opportunity for conquest. That is why they are here now. Self-servers prey on the weak and vulnerable: oppressors need victims. You are vulnerable to victimization by them because of circumstances on your planet now, not because you, as a people, are prone to victimization. That is an important point, which the negatives are overlooking.

The Greys' dishonesty is creating problems for those in your government who have to deal with them. They have assumed that the Greys are capable of making and keeping agreements. They don't realize that negotiation and compromise are not in the Greys' repertoire of behaviors. The Greys do not believe in negotiation or compromise. They think that whoever compromises is weak. They are not letting you know this, of course. But it is clear in their dealings with you. They play your negotiation and treaty games only because they can manipulate you this way, because of your trust.

This is another common tactic of service-to-self and one way they manage to victimize others. They take advantage of their good will and trust, as if to try to teach them not to be good or trusting. In fact, they feel a duty to teach servers the foolishness of their path, and they often succeed temporarily. That most servers go back to serving and trusting others is simply proof to self-servers that servers are not very clever.

It is not easy to convey to you what self-servers are like, because they are different to the core. Nevertheless, they are as cherished by the Creator as any other creation, and their path has its purpose. Self-servers provoke the conflict that so successfully propels evolution. (*Someone* has to play the villain!) It also develops the intellect very effectively. Self-servers develop cleverness that would be admirable if not applied to such devious ends. What it does not develop is attunement to Divine Will. However, from the Creator's perspective, that comes soon enough. The Creator is willing to allow its creations to choose service-to-self as a temporary path.

The Greys have cleverly manipulated your government to do their bidding. They managed to get the government to build them underground bases in the region where Utah, New Mexico, Arizona, and Colorado meet. This explains the many UFO sightings there. A number of Greys were living there and working in laboratories your government built for them, until your government destroyed them recently. Government laboratories were there as well, but they were separate from the Greys' facilities.

There the Greys were carrying out genetic and other experiments in exchange for supplying the U.S. government with technological information. The technology given you so far, however, has either been flawed, useless, or dangerous. Some of it has helped you to build nuclear weapons. These are the same weapons they hope you will destroy yourselves with, in fighting them.

The rest of the technology has all been a sham. They would not give you anything that would help you become stronger, healthier, or happier. On the contrary, they want the opposite for you, although they pretend otherwise. Your scientists are dupes for new technology, and the Greys have used their greed against them. The scientists working on this top secret project imagined they would make discoveries for which they would receive global recognition. However, when this all comes out, they will be seen as accomplices in a traitorous plot with the Greys or — at best — patsies.

These scientists were living under the illusion that they were doing something to strengthen your country's position in the world. Notice, we did not say they believed they were serving humanity. They were (and are) playing the game of "Whoever Has the Best Technology in the World Wins." In this way, they are not so different from the Greys. Both have been playing games of power.

This is not mentioned to indict these few scientists, but to point out a serious problem within the scientific establishment in general. Science serves power and money, when it should serve humanity. Science has fallen into the hands of self-servers, who create projects to serve the cause of power rather than people. This is why science has been more successful in developing weapons than free, safe energy, for instance. This also is why science has opposed spirituality rather than served it.

Self-servers have invaded science, because scientific knowledge has so much potential for power and because many self-servers have the intellects to excel in this area, especially service-to-self Star People and Walk-ins. We are not implying that all scientists are self-servers, only that a large proportion of self-servers are in this field.

Of course many, many servers are in this field, as well. However, the self-servers have set up the rules, which say ethics is apart from science. Even the servers have bought this. But if any field should be guided by ethics, science should. If not, mass destruction can result, which has happened repeatedly in civilizations all over the universe. Those who have fallen this way rarely repeat this mistake in future lives, and usually spend lifetimes trying to teach others what they learned. Like the Zetas, many of the extraterrestrials involved with you today were responsible for massive destruction and are now balancing this by trying to save you from the same fate.

The Greys have manipulated your government another way. They received permission from your government to use unconsenting human subjects in their experiments. They promised to inform your government of who they selected and for what purpose, but they have not upheld this agreement. They have abducted many more people and caused more harm to them than your government would ever have allowed. Had anyone else acted so deceitfully and injuriously, war would have been waged against them — but not against the Greys. They have your government over a barrel, and they know it.

Your government never agreed to allow the Greys to abduct children and kill them, or kill *anyone* for that matter! Yet the Greys have done this repeatedly. Your government knows this, but doesn't know what to do about it. This puts them in a particularly bad position with the citizens of the United States, who expect their government to protect them — not to make secret treaties and be conned.

When this comes out, your government won't look good, which is all the more reason for those involved to remain silent. Besides, those in charge cannot see how telling the public will do anything but aggravate the situation. They don't realize they have extraterrestrial allies waiting to come to their defense once they choose to be open about what is going on. The positives are only waiting for a readiness on the part of your government and people in general before announcing their presence. This time is bound to come soon, because the Greys have been tightening the screws.

Your government finally retaliated by destroying the Greys' underground base and laboratory after they continued to demand more supplies, laboratory space, and subjects. Until then, no one was willing to take a leadership role within this top secret project. It is understandable that your government did not take a stand sooner when it felt technologically overpowered by the Greys. Those in control have no way of knowing how little power the Greys have. The stand the government should take now is not against the Greys, but for honest disclosure of what has been going on over the past forty years.

Disclosure of the government's dealings with the Greys would do two things: elicit the positive extraterrestrials' aid and allow your government to learn about the whole extraterrestrial situation. The government's understanding of the situation is based mostly on its interaction with the Greys; however, the Greys are only a small part of the picture. If people decided to investigate this openly and objectively, much more would come to light, especially with the positive extraterrestrials' help.

Your government is learning an important lesson about service to the people and about secrecy. For the government to carry on in such secrecy shows a lack of trust in democratic principles and a disrespect for democratic values. It contends that a few people know what is best for society. This is not true in matters of security any more than in other matters. Self-servers within government have used the excuse of national security to manipulate your institutions for their own benefit. Much too much of your government operates secretly. This must end if you are to be a truly free and democratic society. The people must adjust the laws to protect themselves from self-servers in government: the enemy is among you!

Of course, this has always been true. There have been self-servers within even the noblest of organizations. Since they are so all-pervasive, all servers should be aware of the signs of service to self:

The first sign is a preoccupation with power, which usually translates into a push for a hierarchical structure. Sometimes hierarchy is necessary, but hierarchies only work when headed by servers. Keeping self-servers from attaining the top positions in an organization requires strong, aggressive servers. Unfortunately, self-servers are usually more motivated than servers to capture positions that mean increased power and money. As a result, corruption is nearly always the companion of hierarchical structures.

Another sign of service-to-self is secrecy. Once a hierarchical structure is in place, self-servers create other ways to distance the top positions of the hierarchy from the rest. This is usually done through closed meetings, secret assignments, and secret agents. Secret agents are needed to carry out secret assignments and to infiltrate the lower ranks, to make sure their cover is working. This enables them to make suggestions about how to maintain the desired illusion. As insidious as this sounds, this is common practice among governments. People even condone their government's covert activities! If self-servers had their way, no one would even know secret agents existed. Not only governments operate this way, these days: even large corporations have their secret plans and sleuths.

Another sign of service-to-self is deception. Whatever plan they have always includes deception. This is because self-servers are working against the values of society and they know it. They know that if people knew what they were doing, they would be stopped. Self-servers are arch criminals; they will break any law to accomplish their ends. They do this not only because laws get in their way, but because they believe in following their own law, which reads: "If you can do it, then you should."

UFO groups already know what we have revealed about the Greys. They need encouragement to pursue their investigations and to continue to pressure the government for disclosure, which is one of our purposes in writing this. It is time for the public to know what the government knows, and the sooner the better. The Greys won't stop what they are doing until they are exposed. Furthermore, they won't take aggressive action against you for exposing them. That is not how they operate. Besides, they know they cannot control you with weapons alone.

If, at the very least, your government disclosed the evidence concerning extraterrestrial spacecraft, it would be in a much better position. Government secrecy and deception fall right into the Greys' hands. The Greys' game will be over when the secrecy is. Your government doesn't trust this, or it would have disclosed what it knows sooner. Those in a position to reveal the secrets are frightened and choosing to pass the responsibility on to someone else, rather than risk retaliation from the Greys. Fortunately, several groups are trying to get the government to open its files and make the evidence concerning UFOs and extraterrestrials public.

Self-servers like the Greys control others by fear, and by breaking them down mentally and emotionally. They understand that a permanent conquest cannot be accomplished with weapons alone. They understand that true subjugation occurs only when subjects submit psychologically and emotionally to their oppressors. Therefore, they consider themselves victorious only after they have subjugated people spiritually. That is their real goal. When they have succeeded in creating victims, then they know they have won.

Subjugation through technology alone would be a temporary victory and an ineffective means to the Greys' ends. It creates heroes and martyrs, which is not what the Greys want. Self-servers want victims: that is, people who believe they are powerless against their oppressors in every way. Technological warfare only proves technological superiority, not spiritual superiority. Self-servers want to win others over to their path. They are crusaders who are not satisfied with bodies, only with souls.

The Greys are not ready for an open confrontation. Their weapon is not ready yet: the ingredient that will keep people in a constant state of fear. That is how they plan to overtake you. This is probably the only thing that would work on a planet like yours, which is not inclined toward victimization and which has your degree of intellectual development. You have had enough practice with your own self-servers to be wise to their tactics, so you are not as vulnerable as you may think. Because of this, the Greys have had to come up with this way to control you. And it is an excellent idea, one that could work. The only flaw in their plan is the lack of time. They will not have time to develop this weapon before they are exposed and conquered themselves.

The Greys cannot imagine this occurring. They don't see failure as a possibility. In part, this is because they feel invincible and underestimate the positives' power, but also because they don't understand your culture. They don't realize you have an excellent capacity for worldwide cooperation and communication. They don't believe your nations can cooperate, because they haven't seen it. However, if your planet was known to be under extraterrestrial threat, the Greys would find out just how well you can cooperate! This is another reason secrecy is working for the Greys. If the Greys' activities were exposed, your planet would have a reason to unite. Under these circumstances, even warring nations would cooperate.

The Greys' projects will be cut short just in time, because they will be exposed before they can complete them. After they have been exposed, the positives will see to it that they leave your planet, but not before offering them whatever help they can. Nevertheless, it will be too late to save their race. Had the Greys allowed the positives to help them earlier, they might have had a chance to save themselves. No one is opposed to the Greys borrowing your genetics to save their race or to their survival. So,

had they agreed to certain conditions for being here and
to leaving after they had received what they came for, they
would have been welcomed and helped. No one is surprised, however, that they refused those conditions and
the aid.

The Greys are working at cross purposes to the
Confederation. The Confederation (a group of servers that
govern the evolution of planets like yours, in this sector of
the universe) has set up guidelines to ease the transition of
your planet from third- to fourth-density. It allows only
certain activities and prohibits others seen as detrimental.

The Greys have been allowed to carry on, even though
their intentions are to undermine this transition, because
the Confederation sees some advantage in their playing a
part in the drama unfolding now on your planet. It sees
no harm in the Greys playing the villain for the time being.
The Greys are adding another dimension to this time in
history and bringing certain lessons to bear.

We have already mentioned some of these lessons: the
inappropriateness of secrecy in a democratic system, how
deception can be as effective as actual weapons, how
service-to-self operates, and the destructiveness of nuclear
weapons. The Greys' biggest contribution, however, will
be helping you come together as one people. The
Confederation is allowing the Greys to play the role of
Earth's enemy as a means for uniting your planet. Global
unity is a major feature of the Golden Age ahead, and this
is one way of provoking this. A common enemy has served
this purpose, time and time again, for other civilizations at
a similar point in their evolution.

The Greys can play this role without being the victor.
The positives won't let them be the victor, but they will let
them play this role. After your experience with the Greys,
you will see your world differently. Just as the pictures of

Earth brought back by the astronauts changed how you saw Earth, so will this experience change you. After this, your eyes will be opened to a new view of the universe. You will have "lost your virginity," and entered into the age of interplanetary existence.

PART II: PREPARING FOR CONTACT

Part II is about how your society and how humanity as a whole might be affected when you are at last approached openly by extraterrestrials. It will provide some guidelines for discriminating and for understanding alien intelligences. What are you to believe? What can you trust? How do you protect yourselves and your interests? How might you be benefited by such a meeting? How might you be harmed? Such a meeting will raise many questions and will shake up every institution and belief system on the planet. You need to be prepared for this meeting so that you can respond with clear thinking but, more importantly, with a clear heart. Your minds will not serve you as well as your hearts — that is, your intuition and feelings — in determining your responses and best courses of action. You will be dealing with highly intelligent but not necessarily spiritually advanced beings. Furthermore, even spiritually advanced beings may not have a thorough enough understanding of you as a species to guide or lead or even help you. You will have to proceed carefully in your interactions with extraterrestrials and not take anything at face value. You will have to "feel" your way through your interactions with them to determine for yourselves what is right or wrong for you, and what is truth or fiction.

We not only hope to save humanity some difficult lessons by raising these questions, we also hope to help you know yourselves as interplanetary beings. It is time for you to move your sights beyond your planet and to begin to see yourselves as belonging not only to Earth but to a larger universe, or at least to the nearest segment of that universe. You are going to meet your neighbors soon, some of whom you will like better than others. Your cooperation and tolerance will be stretched by this, more so than ever before.

So while you are undergoing a shift in consciousness, which will be most intense over the next decade, you will also be introduced to alien humanoids. All this happening in the midst of massive global changes will, indeed, transform the world you live in. It will be transformed, however, primarily because the events in the world and the reunion with your galactic family will jar you into changing how you organize your world and how you think.

The shift in consciousness will be part of this change — and essential to it — by supporting new choices and helping you navigate these times successfully. But the physical changes and events of these years also will be crucial in motivating you to recreate your world's structures and institutions. Without an obvious and pressing need for change, you might simply enjoy this rise in consciousness and continue to live as you always have. But because the situation in which you find yourselves is critical, you will choose to make drastic changes, which might be impossible without the accompanying change of consciousness.

So, if you find yourself cursing the natural disasters and other difficulties you encounter in this decade, please remember that they are part of the process that will bring humanity to a new era and a new world. Many of the old structures must completely disappear before the new can arise. You know how this works in your own lives: periodically, many of you undergo radical changes and recreate your lives anew. This is what the Earth is doing in this decade. And, by necessity, certain structures, attitudes, behaviors, and beliefs must pass away.

SERVERS AND SELF-SERVERS IN THE WORLD TODAY

Both the servers and the self-servers involved with you—incarnate and otherwise—are part of your galactic family. The self-servers are vying with the servers for control of your planet, although the servers don't see it this way. The servers are here to serve you and help you integrate the polarities on your planet. They don't wish to eliminate the extraterrestrial self-servers or the ones incarnate on Earth. They understand that Earth is serving as a place where the polarities are to be integrated.

Your galactic family has tried to integrate the positive and negative polarities in many other locations in your quadrant of the universe, but to no avail. On some planets the negative pole has prevailed, while on others the positive pole has prevailed. But none have achieved a balanced integration of the positive and the negative. This is possible and it is being attempted on Earth now. Earth may or may not succeed. We believe it will. If it doesn't, it is still unlikely to become a service-to-self planet.

Because of the servers' commitment to integration, rather than dominance of one or the other pole, they have been allowing the self-servers to operate freely on Earth. For the same reason, they will also not allow the self-servers to overrun Earth. For those wondering why the servers are allowing the self-servers to harm people and stir up trouble, this is your answer. The self-servers' activities are part of your growth and, specifically, your evolution toward integration.

As you know, growth in a world of polarities is often painful. This pain can be minimized by a philosophy that reframes the painful experience, one that brings understanding to it. Pain also can often be avoided through intelligent action and informed choices. So, although your growth toward integration necessitates some pain, it need not cause great suffering. Suffering occurs when understanding is absent. We hope to provide some of the understanding you will need.

Many others also will be working to alleviate your suffering. But some, including incarnate self-servers, will be striving to create more. Self-servers enjoy creating suffering, because it is evidence of their victory, their superiority. They are not ashamed of this; it is their nature to create suffering. This doesn't excuse them. The point is that individuals like this do exist, and servers must realize this. Self-servers think and feel differently than servers.

This will be all the more apparent as the polarization on Earth increases. This intensification of the battle between Good and Evil, if you will, is being caused not so much by unevolved incarnate self-servers, but by evolved ones. They are the ones who will really baffle you. You are already aware of some of them. Saddam Hussein is the most prominent one today, but others will come into power in this decade.

Some of the incarnate servers' biggest mistakes may come from assuming that self-servers think like they do.

Servers give others the benefit of the doubt and second chances. This plays right into the self-servers' hands. They are thrilled that you are so naïve and easily manipulated. Servers err on the side of acceptance, and that slack is what self-servers use to hang them.

We don't mean to sound negative. But this happens repeatedly in your world, and only by becoming aware of this will you learn to handle the self-servers. In dealing with them, you must be firm and unwavering. You must assume the worst motives and intentions, and stand up to them with every bit as much commitment to good as they have to evil.

The belief that "turning the other cheek" is the way to combat evil has allowed evil to grow. Evil doesn't stop when you turn the other cheek: it strikes you on the turned cheek or finds someone else to bully. You know this, which is why you have built up such great arsenals and why you have needed them, or at least needed the enemy to believe you have them. In saying this, we are not insinuating that the Soviet Union was the Evil Empire. Self-servers as well as servers exist in every country and government. But you in the United States understood the necessity of protecting your sovereignty from those who would take it away from you.

This buildup of arms has been necessary, but it has harmed your natural resources and depleted your economy. The irony is that one nuclear bomb would have been enough. Once you developed nuclear weapons, the buildup of arms became a farce. Now you are concerned about nuclear weapons falling into the hands of people like Saddam Hussein. More nuclear bombs is not the answer. What is the answer, then?

The answer is you must outsmart the self-servers at their own game. You must find ways to anticipate their maneuvers and frustrate them. To do this, you must understand how their minds work.

To self-servers, life is a game of power. They care about nothing more. They don't care who is harmed in their struggle for power, because power is always worth it to them. They don't care how long it takes to get power either, because they have no other motivation for living. They are ruthless and relentless. They are like bulldozers, bulldozing their way through life toward their goal of power.

They don't have moral precepts that define or limit their striving for power. Any morals to which they do give lip service (usually to manipulate others) can always be bent to serve their god: power. When power is everything, then power is one's moral code. They don't see what they do as immoral. They see it as honoring what they believe in: power. Fighting for what they value is as moral to them as fighting for what you value is to you. Power is their entire reason for being, just as love is for others. Self-servers have values just as servers do, but they are opposite ones. Servers think of self-servers as being able to do what they do because they rationalize it, but self-servers don't need to rationalize. They have their own rationale for living, and it doesn't include the same moral standards as for servers.

Servers call some self-servers sociopaths, but this term applies more to unevolved self-servers, particularly ones who have been psychologically damaged in previous lives and who are still damaged. Sociopaths are a less clever variety of self-server than the self-servers like Saddam Hussein, to whom we are referring. Evolved self-servers are far more dangerous, because their ambitions know no bounds and often include power over entire populations or areas of the globe. Evolved self-servers have evolved on service-to-self planets and have intelligence, talents, and (often) psychic abilities to use to achieve their ends.

We have said that a buildup of arms was necessary and that it has led to the possibility of nuclear weapons falling into the hands of self-servers. The situation in which you find yourselves was predictable and inevitable, and one in which many other worlds before you have found themselves. This situation has intensified the polarization. The weapons you have developed allow you to play out the battle between Good and Evil on a very large and destructive scale.

This would not be so complicated if there were distinct sides. But the servers and self-servers are distributed across the globe. The self-servers are stirring up trouble wherever they are. The situation is not as simple as the good countries verses the bad countries (although during the Cold War you acted this way). War, corruption, greed, violence, and horror are all over the world. The enemy is among you, and how do you protect yourselves against that? Your arsenal of weapons is virtually useless when the enemy is both within your country and scattered throughout the countries of your allies.

Much of the confusion in the world is created by just that: your enemies are no longer clear-cut. It was simple when you could focus on the Soviet Union and communism as the fiend, but such simplistic definitions no longer hold. The situation is further complicated by trade alliances and business interests in countries formerly considered unfriendly. One thing certain is that it is not "business as usual." There is nothing usual about these times. The situation calls for a new vision, a vision of yourselves as a global society. Only then will you be able to deal with the undermining influences of the self-servers.

By unifying and organizing the world governments, you have a chance to balance (not eliminate) the evil in the world, if the world government you create (and its leaders) are committed to service and humane values. Right now, the self-servers are having a field day, because you are not taking a proactive stance toward them. You are letting them define what is happening in the world. You are responding to them instead of demanding that they comply with your standards. This is what must change. The servers must be the ones defining history. They must be the ones in charge — the ones in power. We will give you an example.

When Saddam Hussein invaded Kuwait in August of 1990, the United Nations mobilized to deal with him. In doing this, the United Nations became empowered, after having been a fairly ineffectual organization. However, had the United Nations been strong and had the powers in the world been less reliant on oil — a product controlled by and benefiting certain self-servers — the Gulf War might have been avoided. The lack of global organization and the infiltration of self-servers into the governments of various nations have diffused the servers' power. Servers have either not sought positions of power or not taken charge when in power (as the self-servers have), but that is partly the fault of the nature of servers.

Self-servers are drawn to positions that will give them power. That is why you need an organization like the United Nations that is based on service, not power, and on consensus or democracy, not hierarchy. The servers must organize to prevent the self-servers from taking control. The United Nations' interventions in Kuwait and in Somalia are examples of the kind of interventions such an organization based on service might make. Once the world sees that such an organization is really there for the good of the whole, its power will grow.

The battle between the servers and self-servers is a battle of values. The United Nations asserts humane values and human rights. The self-servers would have an organization based on different values. Their organization would look more like an army. It would be a hierarchy, and it would operate through fear, oppression, and violence. If self-servers were not continually vying for power among themselves, such a military machine probably would already exist.

The servers are at a real advantage in being able to cooperate, which is one reason their values have predominated. Servers also are more plentiful on the planet than self-servers. So, servers are at an advantage and will continue to be. Still, they must actively confront the deteriorating world situation and take steps to remedy it. If they would unite against all who try to oppress and control others, the self-servers would have difficulty implementing their plans.

Because this kind of world unity is now critical to the servers' goals, self-servers are trying to undermine the move toward a world government by saying this is part of the Antichrist's plan. What better way to stop the servers than to link the Antichrist (and all this has come to mean) to the positive and natural course for the world today? The last thing self-servers want is world unity around democratic and humane values. They are well aware of the potential for good this holds. They know that world unification is key to creating a new world order in the most positive sense. They are using fear in the form of stories about the Antichrist to slow progress toward world unity. Many servers have bought their message of fear and are being manipulated by this to undermine the creation of a better world.

The self-servers have been very busy spreading fearful stories about what is to come. They want people to believe that the Dark Forces are very powerful and that the Earth is on an inevitable course of destruction. If people believe this, they are likely to either withdraw from the world, seek satisfaction in pleasures, or preach about the end of the world, but they are unlikely to take constructive action for change. That is what the self-servers want. They don't want you to transform yourselves or the planet; they want you to believe that it is too late for that. Beware of anyone with a message like that. And beware of anyone whose message evokes fear, hopelessness, and despair. These are the weapons of self-servers.

The self-servers have constructed a story of conspiracy that has been spread and repeated so many times that it has taken on a life of its own. The story claims that a few bankers and industrialists have been controlling world affairs covertly for generations. What better way to lead people to believe that their lives are not their own nor their governments responsive to them? What better way to breed fear, hopelessness, and distrust of government? By undermining the people's trust in government, the hope is that people will disengage themselves from politics and their responsibilities as citizens. This would leave government to the self-servers in power. They would like nothing more than to be left alone to play their power games. Fortunately, as apparent from the 1992 presidential election campaign, most people are not apathetic, and grassroots movements are more alive than ever. Fortunately, the conspiracy theory has only taken root in a minority of minds.

Much of the information about conspiracy has come from channels and psychics who have served as vehicles for the self-servers without realizing it. The same story is being repeated to various channels and psychics, so it appears to have some credibility. After all, the more something is repeated, the more believable it becomes. So, a story that started out as unbelievable has become believable to many, even some very discriminating people.

One reason even some highly educated people have become convinced of a conspiracy and other falsehoods is that self-servers have other ways (besides through channels and psychics) to persuade people of these ideas. Ideas can be implanted through dreams and intuition, and memories can even be created. These are some of the activities in which nonphysical self-servers are engaged, while many incarnate self-servers as well as servers are being used as vehicles for these ideas.

Discerning truth from fiction is difficult with the intellect alone. Besides, self-servers are very clever; they can easily outsmart people intellectually. To discern truth from fiction, intuition is needed. Discernment will become much easier in the future when the vibration of the planet has increased. There will still be self-servers then, but they will not be heeded or given power as they are now.

Not everyone is equally intuitive, and even those who are are sometimes swayed by their own issues and opinions. Some take pleasure in the idea of conspiracy, because it confirms their belief that evil prevails in the world. Those who are unhappy may find some comfort in this belief, because it takes the responsibility off of them to find happiness. After all, who can be happy in a world overrun by evil? Others like the drama and intrigue of a conspiracy. Others use it as an excuse to complain, without doing anything to change things. Complaining is much easier than fighting for what is right. Besides, how can you fight a hidden enemy like the conspirators? They have been carrying on for decades with impunity. They must be very clever and powerful — probably omnipotent by now (or so the argument goes)!

All of this must seem confusing to you, and it is. That is the point. The self-servers are creating so many stories, particularly through channels, that it is hard to know what to believe. As many falsehoods as truths are coming through channels today. Most of them are unsuspecting servers who have given themselves over to a message that they believe has importance. They feel a duty to convey what they are receiving to others. This sense of duty is present in all channels, whether they are serving the servers or not. So, this cannot be the measure of whether something is true or not. Just because a channel feels a strong commitment to channeling something doesn't give it validity. So, how can you tell truth from fiction?

The first question to ask after hearing or reading about something is how it makes you feel. We are not talking about whether it makes you happy or sad, but how it makes you feel inside. Do you feel a sick or sinking feeling upon hearing it? Do you feel afraid, hopeless, despairing, powerless? These are signs that the information is coming from a negative source.

Even messages of warning from positive sources will not convey a sense of hopelessness. They leave you feeling that you can do something to change the outcome if you don't like it. What, after all, would be the purpose of any message of doom if you could do nothing about it? Servers don't give people messages about things they can't do anything about, only about things they can.

Self-servers, on the other hand, offer messages about things you can do nothing about. They may even tell you what to do to avert it, but that would never be enough. You sense this and end up feeling fearful and powerless. For example, a story is circulating of an invasion of the Reptilians, a seven-foot reptile-like race of extraterrestrials. They are said to be landing by the millions soon. Those who received this message were told to surround the Earth with Light, in defense of themselves.

We don't deny the value of surrounding the planet with Light, but people have been doing this for years. Is it reasonable to conclude that this could stop such an invasion? Even if it could, could you count on enough people doing this? It is useful to question why this information was given. Extraterrestrial servers would not give information like this, because it would serve no purpose; it would only instill fear. But instilling fear is exactly what the self-servers want.

Another question to ask when trying to discern truth from fiction is whether or not the information is rational. Just because information about extraterrestrials deals with the unknown does not mean to suspend common sense in evaluating it. For instance, is it reasonable to believe, as some people claim, that the moon already was colonized by the U.S. and the Soviet Union when the U.S. landed there in 1969, or that Mars also is already colonized? Is it really possible that such secrets could be kept from the public — and why would they be? The believers say that these secret activities are part of a plot devised jointly by the negative extraterrestrials and the global conspirators. The negatives would certainly like you to believe they could pull off such a ruse.

Many who believe in extraterrestrial life, believe everything that comes their way. But believing everything is the flip side of believing nothing; neither is discriminating. Falsehoods are being perpetrated for various reasons, some for simple self-interest and others for broader goals. In your transition from planetary to interplanetary beings, you are very vulnerable to trickery. Certain extraterrestrials have come here to take advantage of this. Don't believe everything. Even if someone else you respect is totally convinced of something, decide for yourself what is true.

It should not be too hard not to believe everything when so much of the channeled information is contradictory.

After reading contradictory information from various channels, you are forced to conclude that someone is wrong, or maybe everyone is. More likely, some of what every channel says is correct and some isn't, with some channels being more correct than others. So, it is not as simple as finding out which channels are right and which ones are wrong. Don't fall into the trap of concluding that a channel or a particular article or book is all true or all false. More likely there is some of both, and you must determine for yourself what is true and what is false. Remember, the self-servers are trying to confuse you so that you don't know what to believe. Therefore, they will mix their fiction and fear with truth, and they will speak in the loving terms of servers.

You cannot count on loving phrases as proof of the validity of something. The self-servers know you are vulnerable to feeling loved and valued. They sprinkle their messages with as much love as the servers, sometimes more. The difference is that they use loving words to manipulate you into trusting them, while servers convey love less through their words and more through a feeling sense that underlies the material. Beware of gushy expressions of love and phrases designed to endear you. Most highly developed servers convey their love in less direct ways.

Not only do self-servers offer a mixture of truth and falsehoods disguised in loving words, but channels often channel a mixture of information from both servers and self-servers. Self-servers are able to interfere with the servers' communications to channels under certain circumstances, particularly when the channel is tired or ill. This also happens to channels who are not operating fully in the Light because of negative thoughts and feelings. When channels are under stress, temporarily overcome with negative emotions, or living daily with negativity in their environment or mental habits, they may draw self-servers to them. Channeled material is still an important source of information, however, and should not be discarded altogether. Servers are using channels today more than ever to bring in the new ideas needed to transform people and the global situation. New inventions and ideas, creative inspirations, spiritual understanding, and uplifting truths are coming through channels today, as they always have. But there also is more interference today from self-servers than ever before, because these times are so critical.

If you are a channel or if you are interested in benefiting from channeled material, here are some suggestions for protecting yourself from negativity and falsehoods:

1. How does the material feel intuitively to you? Does it uplift and excite you, or does it make you feel fearful and despairing?

2. How does the channel feel to you? Try to tune in to the channel's energy, to his or her consciousness. However, don't judge a channel by outward appearances, which can be deceiving.

3. Does the material make sense? Is it logical? Are the arguments substantive? Does one idea follow from another? Use your intellect as you would in critiquing information of any kind.

4. Pay attention to how you feel as you read or hear each sentence. Be willing to reject some of the information without rejecting all of it.

5. Raise your own vibration through meditation and commitment to service, and you will attract helpful, positive information and people: like attracts like. If you don't

want to be exposed to negative material, live in love, joy, acceptance, and peace, and avoid fear, hatred, despair, guilt, and shame. Self-servers are attracted to negativity.

THE FIRST CONTACT

The positives have a general plan for introducing themselves to you. The negatives' plans concerning this are unpredictable, but will be known to the positives as events unfold. How this drama is enacted will be influenced by the negatives since the positives will be (in part) reacting to them. The positives will have to work around the negatives' activities.

When the first open contact is made, it will shake the world. People will not know what to think. Even those who have accepted the idea of extraterrestrials will be shocked, as they face the need to further integrate this. They will, of course, be less shaken than those who have not believed in extraterrestrials.

The positives will not announce their presence until the non-believers are in the minority. The positives are waiting for this time, because they know how disruptive an announcement like this can be to a world. They know that if at least half the population is psychologically prepared for a meeting, then the announcement stands a chance of being acknowledged rather than ignored, laughed at, or repressed.

There have been times in other worlds when extraterrestrial contact was not accepted for what it was. The people refused to believe what was before their eyes and either denied or repressed the experience. As you can imagine, they could only do this for so long before they were forced to accept what they saw. Nevertheless, undoing denial or repression can be painful and time-consuming for a population, which is why we hope to avoid this.

If this were to happen, it would not be unlike your current situation, where those who have not denied the experience are laughed at or persecuted, and those who regain their memory are traumatized by their remembrances and *then* laughed at or persecuted. Although some in your world are still bound to deny or repress the experience, if most do not, the encounter will be considered a success. Mass denial and repression are what we want to avoid, because this would cause undue pain and delay the achievement of our goals.

We anticipate three possible reactions to the announcement that extraterrestrials are here on Earth:

1. The announcement will not receive media coverage. Instead, either the government or others who feel they are acting in the people's best interests will try to cover it up.

2. The announcement will be covered by the media (but as a joke), dismissed, and then covered up.

3. The announcement will be taken seriously and all activities between the government and the extraterrestrials will be handled openly and honestly.

Obviously, the media will be a key player in the first official contact. The positives have every intent of including the media and inviting them to interview them. They believe this is the only way that mass acceptance will occur.

They have seen what has happened when media coverage has not been allowed and activities have been kept secret.

The desire for media coverage is one of the most obvious differences between the positive and the negative extraterrestrials. The negatives have shunned media coverage, because it would interfere with their covert activities. The positives, on the other hand, will use the media to accomplish their goals and to expose the negatives' activities. They will use it to unite the world, not divide it as the negatives have been trying to do.

The media is a powerful force for good, although you have not always used it that way. The positives will show you new ways of using your telecommunications systems to the world's advantage. They will help you set up telecommunications throughout the world so that even very remote areas of the globe can be linked to the rest of humankind. This will allow for more and better educational opportunities and improved understanding between nations. This could, of course, also be misused. For instance, who determines what will be broadcast and will commercials be allowed? The extraterrestrials have guidance to offer you on this and many other subjects. They have been through this transition before on other worlds.

Sometimes you will receive conflicting advice even from the positive extraterrestrials, since there are many varieties, each with their own point of view. You will have to sift through their advice and decide for yourselves what to do. You will need very wise leaders for this, but they are already appearing. The problem with the positives will not be that they may deceive you, because servers don't do this, but that their advice may not be appropriate. However, you will have to be on the lookout for negatives posing as positives and guard against their deceptions and bad advice.

You will not be able to count on the positives pointing out the negatives to you, either. They will give you clues, but they believe you must learn to discriminate and make your own choices — and mistakes.

When the first contact is made, it is likely to stop the world temporarily, as news of this passes from one person to the next and is processed. There will be as many reactions to this news as there are people, since each person will have individual feelings and ideas about what this will mean. For instance, the toy maker, who never even believed in extraterrestrials, may be elated at the prospect of a new line of toys depicting the various extraterrestrials. The minister, to whom most turn in times of crisis, may be having his own crisis of belief. And the science fiction writer, who always wanted to meet an extraterrestrial, may question his past works or future livelihood. Everyone touched by this will react according to his or her own situation, needs, desires, and viewpoint. The only constant will be that everyone's image of the future will be in question.

Some people will be more comfortable having their view of themselves and life upturned than others. Some will be thrilled, while others will be equally frightened. You will see all manner of extremes as people struggle to come to grips with the shock. Rarely does a race have anything as shocking happen as meeting with an alien race. You know how native peoples in your own world were affected by this. Your meeting with extraterrestrials will be no less upsetting to the world than this.

Once such a meeting is made, as you know, there is no turning back of time. History is changed from that point forward. It will be up to you to see that it is a history you are proud of. The positives' intent is to help you build a better world. If they didn't believe this was possible now, they would not be here. They are here to help you transition to a fourth-density world, one that functions more harmoniously and more fully in the Light.

One thing that will be different about meeting the positive extraterrestrials than meeting people from another culture is the difference in development. We are not only referring to intellectual differences but differences in spiritual evolution. Many will feel as if they are meeting gods, because of the enormous love, acceptance, peace, and wisdom exuded by the positives. An encounter with positives is not at all like an encounter with negatives, which can be a terrifying and depleting experience. Nevertheless, not everyone will feel uplifted by the positives. Some people have blocks that will prevent them from experiencing this. So, not everyone will have the same reaction. Conflicts will undoubtedly arise from the various reactions to the positives, but most people will be open enough to feel the positives' love and wisdom.

Those who do feel the positives' love will instinctively trust them. They will evoke feelings of worship from some people, but no one will be encouraged to worship them. The positives are here to teach you of your own godhood, not make themselves gods. They have been your gods before, but they come as equals now, as members of the same family. They are here to reunite you with this family and invite you to take your rightful place in the galaxy.

They will not lord their power over you, tell you what to do, or give you the answers to your problems. They will welcome you into the family, tell you about it, and guide you in functioning more positively in your own world. In helping you improve your relations with each other, they are preparing you for relating to your galactic neighbors. Once you have healed your own world, you will be ready to function as interplanetary beings.

Some of the positives will be very beautiful to you and some hideous. This will cause you to examine your concepts of beauty and the value you have placed on it. It will become apparent that physical beauty is only one form of beauty, as even hideous creatures evoke your love and respect. The ones that are hideous to you will not be introduced to you at first, of course. We understand the allure physical beauty holds for you, as well as what you consider beautiful. Therefore the Pleiadians, who are most like you, will be the positives' first emissaries. Be forewarned, however, that the positives come in all forms and not all are ones you would consider attractive.

Not only do extraterrestrials come in all forms, but some have *no* form! Many of those observing you are nonphysical, but can materialize any kind of a form they wish. They will materialize a form to suit their purposes, most likely a human form that will allow them to intermingle comfortably with you. However, some negatives also can materialize and dematerialize. You can be sure they will use this to their advantage.

Once the positives have announced their presence, the negatives will act more overtly than previously. They are likely to impersonate positives and try to persuade you to take their advice. However, their advice will cause you problems, which is their goal. It is not even that they have distinct goals, except that you not progress. They want your societies to deteriorate and to be overrun with negativity. Then, they believe, they will be able to overpower and rule you. Therefore, anything that will contribute to your demise will do.

The negatives are easy enough to distinguish from the positives, even when they make themselves look like them. They can be distinguished by their behavior, their methods, and their energy. Many of you will be able to feel their negativity, but their behavior and words also will betray them. The negatives will be invested in having you follow their advice, so they will pressure you to take it. They will try to convince you with hype and promises, like any salesperson. So beware of sales pitches. The positives will not be pitching anything. They will offer advice when asked and hold forums on your problems. They will offer solutions without claiming that they are the only ones, and they will not insist you follow them.

The negatives are likely to use fear to convince you to listen to them and adopt their solutions. They will tell you stories of what has happened to other worlds, and what they believe will happen to you if you don't follow their advice. These stories will be false and designed to scare you into doing as they suggest. Their suggestions will aggravate your troubles, not alleviate them. With a little careful thought on your part, you will realize this.

You can trust your intellect to determine what is likely to work or not work in your world, so don't be misled into believing that you are incapable of evaluating the solutions offered you. Any technology offered to you can be understood well enough by your scientists to know whether it is feasible or not. Don't take anyone's word for anything without examining it critically.

You have numbers on your side. Not nearly as many negatives are involved in your world as positives. The negatives are therefore at a disadvantage. They will have difficulty getting your attention, because there will be many others with whom you will be working who will be offering more sensible solutions than the negatives. Still, some people are bound to be duped.

The adage about safety in numbers is good advice when working with extraterrestrials. Working with groups of extraterrestrials will be much safer than working with individuals. The likelihood of being duped will be much less if you make a policy of interacting with groups of them, and within committees of people. That way, you will have the advantage of many people's input and intuition. Furthermore, the orientation of an extraterrestrial is easier to determine with a group of them than individually. A group of negatives is easy to spot, but one negative alone is more difficult to peg. One sure sign is that they don't cooperate well.

Even though you need to be cautious in accepting advice from extraterrestrials, the potential for benefit to your world — technologically and spiritually — from contact with the positives is enormous, and therefore worth the effort and any challenges.

Working with the positives will even be challenging, as working with any different culture or race would be. There are bound to be misunderstandings, hurt feelings, bruised egos, and the usual problems that occur when individuals come together to solve problems. It will help to focus on your shared concern for planet Earth and the welfare of the human race. This will bind you and help you overcome your differences.

You will be willing to overcome your differences, because you each have something to offer the other. Perhaps you have just been thinking of what the positives can do for you, but they also are here for their own purposes. They will be asking things from you as well, and you will have to decide whether you want to help them. The negatives will have requests, too. The positives don't necessarily oppose your fulfilling the negatives' requests, because they believe in the negatives' right to survive.

However, some of the negatives' requests will be false ones, designed to waste your time and resources and distract you from the work of uniting and healing your world. So, you will have to be discriminating even in granting requests for help.

The negatives need not pose a serious threat to your work with the positives. They are likely to cause confusion and teach you something about discrimination, but that will probably be the worst of it. Some material from other channels may contradict this, however. It may speak of diabolical plots, special weapons, invasions, vast numbers of negatives, and so forth. Please remember that the negatives want you to believe that they are powerful and here in great numbers. This increases their power. When you hear stories of negatives that frighten you, remember this.

It would serve no purpose for us to understate the reality. We are not understating the negatives' threat. Those who overstate their threat are being used by those forces, to spread fear. What purpose would it serve for us to understate the situation? What purpose would it serve them to overstate it? These are the kinds of questions you need to ask. Question the motives for what you hear, and ask who is likely to benefit.

The positives will always be honest with you. If there is something they don't want you to know, they will not tell you, and they will probably tell you they cannot tell you. They will not make up an answer to manipulate you. This is a basic guideline of how we operate. The positives may not always be right, however. Their predictions may prove false, but it won't be because they are trying to manipulate you, but because prediction is difficult.

The negatives, on the other hand, will use your desire to know the future to fool and manipulate you. They also will try to get you on the wrong course by dangling something you want in front of you. For instance, they may tell you they have the answer to your energy problem. But when you pursue their solution, you come to a dead end, having wasted precious time and money. You cannot trust the negatives to tell you the truth. They will tell you whatever is in their best interest. Truth has nothing to do with it. Lying is their most common tactic. Of course, they have a way of doing this that draws you in and gives you just enough reason to believe them. They are clever liars.

If you think of the con artists you have heard of, you will have a good idea of how negatives think and operate, but more skillfully and with more technological resources than the best con artists on Earth. Think of how much more vulnerable you are to beings with special powers and technology, how much easier it is for them to fool you. You are especially vulnerable now because your world is unstable. Like con artists, the negatives look for those who are most vulnerable. They take pleasure in kicking people when they are down. In their minds, they are doing them a service by teaching them a lesson they need to learn.

It is good that your society is wising up to con artists, because that will help you deal with the negatives. The adage, "If it's too good to be true, it probably isn't true," is a good one to remember. Con artists and negatives prey on those who want a quick fix or easy way out. But you get what you pay for, and if you're not careful, you won't even get that!

We have examined what to expect after contact is made. Now let's examine how that contact might be made by the positives. Doing this will not only prepare you, but will also help you determine who is contacting you, in the unlikely event that the negatives contact you before the positives. The plan is not set, but we can describe a few ways the positives won't contact you:

We will not disrupt the air waves and make a statement. This would be too sensational and controlling. We will not take control of anything in order to gain your attention, because this sends a message of aggression and dominance. The last thing we want to do is have you feel you are being taken over. For the same reason, we will not flaunt our powers. That would only intimidate you. We don't want you to feel disempowered or frightened. That is key to our plan.

We also will not appear spectacularly on the White House lawn, for many of the same reasons. Drama and splash are not our style, but the negatives'.

We also will not approach anyone in the media without first contacting key people in your government. As much as we will use the media once contact is made, our business is with your government officials, not with the media.

You can expect us to contact the President of the United States, because this is a matter of state, an official greeting on our part to your head of state. It has already been explained why the United States officials are targeted for first contact. How will this meeting with the President be arranged, if not through the media or a dramatic arrival? The Pleiadians will contact someone who can arrange a private meeting with the President. Certain strategies may be used at that time to convince that individual of the Pleiadians' extraterrestrial identity. In the meeting with the President, a means of informing the public will be agreed upon, most likely through an announcement and introduction by the President.

How will the President be convinced of the Pleiadians' identity? We have ways of proving this. And how will he be persuaded to make this announcement, rather than cover up this meeting? We will convince him. The Pleiadians also are prepared to make the announcement by some other means, perhaps through some other official. Other governments will be contacted shortly thereafter, with a similar message of peace and camaraderie.

After the initial contact is made with officials and the public, the positives will work with officials to establish a committee to help us achieve our mutual goals. We will work with you any way you wish and we expect you to formulate goals, as well. We don't expect or desire to dictate even the format of our interactions, but we will make suggestions. We wish to work cooperatively — jointly — with you toward solving your problems, especially the problem of peace. But how this is done will be largely up to you.

The negatives, should they approach you first, will act more dramatically and dictatorially. They may attempt to imitate us, but that is not easy for them. They don't know how to cooperate or negotiate, so this should show. They are bound to be brash, overconfident, clumsy, and insensitive to your feelings and needs. These are things to look out for.

They also are likely to opt for secrecy, rather than honest disclosure of their dealings with officials. This is another sign. Openness and honesty are watchwords of the positives. Deception is difficult in an open atmosphere. Since the negatives will be relying heavily on lies, openness works against them. They will probably have logical reasons for secrecy, but be forewarned that this is not how the positives will operate.

One final word of caution: don't align yourselves with only one group of extraterrestrials. Just as there is safety in numbers, it is wise to remain open to all groups of extraterrestrials. By interacting with all, you will come to know the differences between the positives and the negatives. You will not be able to judge by appearances alone, especially since the negatives are likely to manipulate their appearance to ingratiate you. Each of the extraterrestrial groups has a unique perspective and unique gifts to offer you. By staying open to all of them, you will come to understand them and keep your options open.

APPEARANCES AND OTHER DIFFERENCES

What about appearances? The subject of appearances needs to be approached by considering not only what you *can* tell from appearances, but what you *cannot* tell from appearances, as appearances can be deceiving, especially when dealing with extraterrestrials. In addition, if you are to understand your extraterrestrial relatives, you will have to consider the ways you are different from them, besides your appearance.

One of your first concerns will be learning to tell the Zetas from the Greys. You will recall that they resemble each other, because they originated from the same race and evolved under similar circumstances. There are some differences, however. The most obvious one is that the Greys are generally shorter than the Zetas and lighter in color. The Greys are often whitish-gray, whereas the Zetas tend to be greenish-gray and therefore a bit darker. The differences are subtle but noticeable enough when the two are side by side.

Another difference is in the eyes. The Zetas have a wateriness about their eyes, a softness and depth, like pools of deep water. They give comfort and assurance to humans through their eyes and telepathically, but the Greys do not. The Greys' eyes have a coldness and blackness to them, like the night.

The Greys do not concern themselves with human emotions, which they prefer to ignore. The Zetas, on the other hand, although they also are uneasy with human emotions, try to make humans feel comfortable according to their ideas of this. They may not always respond appropriately, but they do try. Both the Greys and the Zetas are clinical and direct in their manner. But unlike the Zetas, the Greys have a total disregard for feelings.

These are the only clues we can offer, but it shouldn't take you long to learn to distinguish one from the other. Seeing them side by side may not be a common experience, but even a few opportunities like this will be very educational. The Greys will avoid the Zetas whenever possible, however.

Nevertheless, there will be times when the positives and negatives will be involved with you simultaneously. The negatives will work with the positives from time to time because they will need to, to gain your confidence. They will hope to get some of you alone later, to continue their interactions more privately to serve their own ends. The positives will allow the negatives to work with them, and leave it up to you to determine your allegiances.

As long as the negatives are part of a larger group (including positives), they cannot do much harm. But beware of them singling out people and working with them independently. They can spot people's weaknesses, and they will try to use anyone who can be corrupted. They will tempt people with power or whatever else they have a weakness for, in exchange for something they want. Since like attracts like, you will be wise to have only the most impeccable people working on projects with the extraterrestrials. This is one way to safeguard yourselves. However, the negatives will still find ways to work independently with less scrupulous types.

The positives, when they do have forms, are usually in humanoid form, although they may also possess the ability to shape-shift into other forms. On the other hand, some of the negatives (like the Reptilians or "Lizzies," as they are sometimes called) usually resemble animals. So any extraterrestrial in animal form is likely to be a negative, but these negatives will rarely show themselves anyway. The negatives that will show themselves to you will be either the Greys (with whom many of you and your government are already familiar and who may pass as Zetas); the Orions (as Men in Black), who will continue their various missions even after the positives contact you; and the negative Sirians, who can take any form they wish. Because of their ability to shape-shift, the negative Sirians will be the ones to watch. They are likely to imitate Pleiadians and others with whom you will form bonds.

The Pleiadians are very beautiful and may therefore easily win your confidence. But be careful not to be too trusting even of them, because they are the ones the negatives are most likely to impersonate. You will find the positives as a whole very beautiful. Even though they may not be conventionally beautiful to you, they will evoke feelings of love within you, which are translated by you as beauty. The meaning of the expression "love is blind" will never be more obvious than when you meet your galactic comrades.

Love is something the negatives cannot fake, although they try to, at least through words and mannerisms. Your own feelings of love will be your best guide in determining who is who among extraterrestrials. However, this rule of thumb will not work for everyone, since not everyone will be open enough to feel the positives' love. They will not evoke love in everyone.

Some of the humanoids you will meet, both positive and negative, will be tall and others very small. This will challenge your usual associations about large and small. You tend to think of large as better and stronger, and small as lesser and weaker. This is certainly not true in other realms, where size and shape have nothing to do with worth or ability. Size and shape are particularly inconsequential, given that many of the beings you will meet are not bound to their forms but can change form at will.

Your idea of male and female roles also will be challenged. Genders do exist among many of the extra-terrestrials, but others are either androgynous or without gender. You will find that there are many ways to procreate and that your gender roles and identities are specific to you. Each species has their own conception of gender, and the roles are set accordingly.

You will realize in meeting other species how culture-bound you are. There is nothing wrong with this; it is perfectly natural. But exposure to other species will enlarge your concept of yourselves, just as exposure to other human cultures has. What you are about to learn about yourselves, as a result, will transform you over the next few decades. Never has a generation been exposed to so much that is new. This will try you, especially those who are less open-minded or open to change. However, exposure to alien races has a potential for growth equal only to the major leap in consciousness you also will be experiencing. Is there any question that these will be important times?

You will not only have to get used to a vast array of physical differences, but emotional ones as well. Some extraterrestrials, as we have seen with the Zetas and Greys, have no emotions whatsoever. Others have different emotions altogether, while others have emotions like yours but more evolved.

It will become apparent that emotions are only a small part of the makeup of a humanoid, a very small part for some. Humans are used to identifying with their emotions. When they feel sad, they say "I am sad." You will discover in observing other species that your emotions are only a tool that helps you function in the world, a means by which you can know your physical, emotional, social, intellectual, and spiritual needs. Emotions are useful, but they do not make the human! This insight will change your relationship to your own emotions and those of others. Some of you already know this.

You will find that although some alien races have similar emotions, they express them differently. This can be confusing, for instance, when a loud voice expresses caring or a whisper expresses disagreement. These times will demand careful, thoughtful communication, if you are to understand each other on a feeling level. What you do have on your side is that most communication will be done telepathically. This will eliminate many of the ordinary misunderstandings, but not the confusion caused by differences in emotional makeup.

Your intellectual differences will be no small matter, either. All the extraterrestrials you will encounter, both positive and negative, are far beyond you intellectually. They not only use a greater portion of their brains than you, but most have brains that are unlike yours. Those with similar brains, the Pleiadians for instance, will be much easier for you to relate to than others. Those with completely different brains will be alien indeed. Because of this, you will have little interaction with these types. They will perform certain duties behind the scenes and not be players in the drama unfolding on Earth. So, there will be both extraterrestrials known to you, and their helpers, who will remain unknown to you. These helpers are both physical and nonphysical.

Their intelligence puts the extraterrestrials at an advantage. They have studied your culture; some have even observed you for millennia. Many can speak your languages, and those who cannot could learn them in a matter of weeks. Communicating with you in language is hardly an issue, however, because their advanced intelligence allows for telepathy. They know how to stimulate certain centers in your brain, which enables you to receive their telepathic messages without your being telepathic. Therefore, they can communicate with you the same way they communicate with each other.

Misunderstandings still occur in telepathic communication, however. Certain differences create variances in translation of the telepathic communication, causing misunderstandings, although they are infrequent and usually minor. Misunderstandings are more likely to arise from differences in intelligence than from problems with translation. Cultural differences, of course, will also cause some misunderstandings. So you can expect some problems.

Because of their superior intelligence, all extraterrestrials are skillful at anticipating your responses to them and therefore capable of manipulating you. The positives manipulate you as a parent manipulates a child, to evoke a desired response. The difference between this kind of manipulation and that of the negatives is that the positives manipulate situations for your highest good, while the negatives' motives are always self-serving.

This analogy of parent and child is fitting in many respects. The positives have greater reasoning powers, more foresight and wisdom, more skills, and higher emotional development than humans. This makes them well suited to act as parents. Moreover, their advanced spiritual development gives them access to guidance from Spirit about your spiritual plan. Without this, their intelligence and wisdom might be misdirected.

This connection to Spirit is lacking in the negatives and is what makes them so dangerous. It makes them dangerous to themselves, too, because they make choices out of alignment with the Creator. To align with the Creator would mean accepting the Creator's help, which would go against their tenet of self-reliance.

As difficult as it may be for you to imagine what it means to be billions of years more advanced intellectually and emotionally, it is even more difficult for you to imagine what this means spiritually. You understand that spiritual development leads to becoming more like God: more loving, compassionate, and accepting. And you will feel this love, compassion, and acceptance from the positives. However, you still will not understand what they are experiencing — what it is like to be them. You will project your ideas about this on to them, but you will never grasp their experience.

We are telling you this, because we want to put this in perspective for you. They are not like you. Not only are they not human — even if they were, their billions of years of development would still make them unrecognizable to you. So, please be careful about assuming that they are like you. They know what you are like, and they will accommodate you and speak to you in your terms. But this will be for purposes of communication, not because this is how they are.

They are so advanced that they can understand you and interact with you — an entirely alien race — on your terms! They have done this countless times before, in other worlds, and they will do this countless more times. They are carrying out their work here as you carry out your daily business, but their business is unimaginably more complex. This is not intended to elicit your awe or reverence, but to remind you that your understanding of them will be based on your projections, which are a product of your current state of consciousness.

The positives don't expect anything more from you. They understand how you will see them and how you will feel. They know you better than you know yourselves. They know you like a parent knows a child, and they love you like one. The negatives, on the other hand, see you as a lower life form that is useful, sometimes bothersome, and dispensable. They have treated many of you like animals in a laboratory experiment, because you are little more than that to them. The only difference is that you have free will, but they just see that as something to conquer; it challenges them only slightly.

The negatives don't care if you survive as a race. They would prefer you didn't, if it means having Earth. They are open to sharing Earth with you only if they can completely dominate you. That they have succeeded in other worlds reveals how vulnerable some races are to manipulation. They expect you to be equally vulnerable, but you are not that naïve.

The negatives are intelligent, but their lack of empathy limits their intelligence. They don't know how to interact with you, because they can't put themselves in your shoes. Therefore, sometimes they act in ways that appear stupid. As a result, you may underestimate their intelligence. But it is not a lack of intelligence that trips them up; it is a lack of empathy.

They have other character flaws, which will cause them to make mistakes with you. They lose track of the whole picture because of their egocentricity, and they have trouble delaying gratification. They also don't know how to work with others or win their loyalty or confidence. Because the negatives are so unskilled at human relations, the positives are not concerned that most people will be fooled by them. Some people will be, but they are likely to be those who also are "out for themselves."

The negatives will play intellectual games with you, like giving you bogus information. You will think you have been given something very valuable, but it will be meaningless. This has already happened several times to individuals working for your government. This is one of the negatives' favorite tricks. They will also pretend to be doing things that seem important but really aren't. They will go through the motions while you watch, thinking you are observing something important, something you assume will help you solve some problem.

The negatives won't just play with your minds; they will play with your hopes and dreams. They know every dream you have. If you dream of being a famous writer, they will promise to give you something to achieve that. If you dream of winning the Nobel Prize, they will promise a breakthrough formula. What makes this so tricky is that positives also will be working with writers, scientists, educators, politicians, and the like. So it will be up to you to determine what is valuable and what is not, from the extraterrestrials you encounter. Many people will be sent on wild goose chases, while others will receive useful information. You only need to be pure of heart to be a vehicle for the positives. Those who are greedy or power-hungry will be the ones targeted by the negatives.

One of the problems with the disparity in intelligence between you and the extraterrestrials is that you will not be able to fully understand why they are doing what they are doing. We have tried to explain what they will be doing in terms you can understand, given your current paradigm. However, this cannot be fully grasped by you at your current level of consciousness. This is not to belittle you but to caution you not to assume that you understand the extraterrestrials or what they are doing. And because you cannot fully comprehend them, you will have to trust them, or rather learn who to trust.

As a result of your contact with extraterrestrials, you will make a leap in your own intelligence. The positives will show you how to access a larger portion of your brain and teach you things that will stretch your mental capacity.

Your intelligence also will be improved because of the influx of Star People and their progeny. The children of Star People will inherit an increased intelligence. Some will even be geniuses by your standards, whether or not they are Star People themselves. If Star People can influence others by their energy alone, how much more can they influence their children! Thus, the children of Star People will be blessed by greater insight, intelligence, and other talents than normal children. This will eventually affect the intelligence of your entire population.

Star People will be working as bridges between the positives and you to help you integrate the information they give you. Highly intelligent people are needed for this and have incarnated for this purpose. As a result, there are more geniuses on Earth now than ever before, many of them working in the fields of science and mathematics.

You will need them to help you learn to traverse the vast reaches of space, among other things. You have much to learn before you can travel beyond the speed of light.

The positives will not transport you through space regularly. You will not be able to rely on them for this. Rather, they will help you develop your own space technology. Although you will want to travel in your physical state on their ships, this will not be allowed immediately, except for a few individuals and then only on very short trips. Your physiology cannot withstand interdimensional space travel yet. However, many of you have traveled great distances with extraterrestrials, in your astral body during sleep. These trips will continue, because it is one way you are being introduced to the universe and its occupants. Many of you also are serving others during these excursions. You will be shown much of the technology on their ships, but it will take you years before you begin to understand what you have seen.

Genetics is another area in which you will receive extensive help from the positives. Many of your illnesses can be solved by learning to alter genetic information. This is a simple procedure to them, which they will teach you. They may do this in exchange for certain agreements from you. They are most concerned about your living peaceably with each other and eliminating your nuclear weapons. They can make a strong case for dismantling your nuclear weapons, since they can help you achieve whatever you might otherwise achieve through wars and threats. If you are fighting over food or water, for example, they can show you how to produce more food or purify your water. But their condition for helping you will be that you learn to get along.

If the negotiating chip is peace, then you can be sure you are dealing with the positives. The negatives want to see the opposite and will try to inflame your hatreds and disagreements. They may pretend to be giving you a solution to a disease, while actually creating a new one. They, too, will be very interested in genetics experiments. However, you will be the victims, not the beneficiaries. Genetics will be an area you will have to watch closely.

The positives' other agenda is the environment. They will help you create clean energy sources, dispose of toxic waste, manufacture biodegradable materials, improve your agricultural practices, and purify your air and water. They may ask for certain concessions before helping you with these things, particularly peace.

The negatives also may offer you help with the environment, but they will not offer real solutions and they will make demands other than that you live peacefully. They will probably want laboratory space or permission to perform genetic experiments or something else that will serve them, not you. Pay attention to motives. The positives will not be looking for anything for themselves. What they do ask you for will be for the good of the whole. Even the Zetas can carry out their genetics projects without any major concessions from you. They already have Star People and others willingly helping them with their experiments.

Of all the differences between you and the extraterrestrials, the physical ones are bound to be the hardest to adjust to. To prepare you for a face-to-face encounter with the many strange-looking extraterrestrials you are to meet, you will be given an audiovisual recording of each of the extraterrestrial groups involved with Earth. An ambassador of each group will address you on behalf of the others and explain the background, purpose, and role of that particular group in regard to Earth. Eventually, many of them will be walking on your Earth and interacting with you daily. To prepare you for this eventuality, you will meet them first on video.

The first phase of this introduction is already being accomplished through movies and television programs like *Star Trek: The Next Generation* and *Deep Space Nine,* depicting alien beings and human beings working together, not just as adversaries. These shows are no accident.

You will be introduced to a wide variety of beings, so wide that you will become quite used to strange-looking beings. Your eyes will become accustomed to this diversity and you will no longer even think in terms of "strangeness." The attitude to cultivate during this transition is one of open curiosity, innocence, and a determination to look beyond appearances.

Certainly how you see each other and how you evaluate beauty will also be affected. Eventually, you will drop your categories of beautiful and ugly. This may be inconceivable to you now, but it will happen. First your concept of physical beauty will change, then it will disappear. The idea of judging someone by appearances will become ludicrous and unimaginable — but that will be a few centuries from now. Until then, you will struggle with your old ideas of beauty until you finally give them up.

Your encounter with extraterrestrials will require you to give up many of your ideas, and it will bring many new ones into your awareness. It will be impossible to live by the old ideas, which will be antiquated. You will eventually find your way through this morass of change to a new world of greater love and acceptance. These are exciting times ahead, full of wonder and change.

LIVING IN AN INTEGRATED WORLD

The world of the future will be integrated in two ways: the polarities will be integrated and so will the races, including a variety of extraterrestrial races. Let's look first at what it would mean to live in a world where the polarities are integrated.

You already know what this will be like somewhat, because some of you have already integrated the polarities within yourselves. That is where global integration begins: within. Integration on an emotional level means accepting your dark side, your shadow. It means accepting all your "nasty" emotions for what they are — messages about your needs.

Denying your needs leads to depression, anger, resentment, and outbreaks of violence. You now realize that denying anger creates a backlash of violence and hatred, which fuel the cycle of negativity on Earth. Although all negativity will not be erased entirely from your planet, or any planet operating through polarities, the negative pole need not be as prominent as it is today. An integrated society will have less negativity than what exists on Earth today.

Through the cycle of violence — that is, violence breeding more violence — negativity is not only perpetuated but multiplied. This is how the negative pole comes to dominate, as in service-to-self planets. But a cycle of love also is possible: love begets more love. The cycle of love does not eliminate (nor deny) the negative pole any more than the cycle of violence eliminates the positive pole. In an integrated society, the negative pole is balanced against the positive pole, and exists as a foil and a learning device. That is the appropriate role for negativity. Likewise, even on a service-to-self planet, the positive pole remains as a reminder and a call to another kind of action. Thus, both poles remind the other of other possibilities. The presence of these two possibilities gives you a choice of lifestyle: the cycle of violence or that of love.

The cycle of violence is painful, unless you are the oppressor. And even so, the tables are bound to be turned sometime. The cycle of love is always joyful. Why would anyone choose the painful path then? The only ones who willingly choose this are self-servers, because they believe happiness lies in controlling others. However, they are no more happy on this path than their victims, except perhaps fleetingly. The happiness they experience is an illusion, because it does not come from alignment with the Creator. Self-servers believe they have achieved happiness, because they have nothing else to compare it to; they don't know the joy of love.

Furthermore, they will never learn this on their own; the servers will teach them this through the process of integration. Through this process, self-servers learn the role that evil and negativity play for all creation. They learn that it is part of creation, not the whole of it, and they eventually choose to serve. Nevertheless, there will always be others, usually unevolved souls, who will play the part of negativity for a while. So, the only difference between an integrated or integrating society and a service-to-self society is the degree of negativity that exists and the power it has.

Once you have integrated your shadow self, others who have not will be reminders of this side of yourself. Therefore, you will be forced to continue to acknowledge and accept it. In an integrated society, self-servers act as reminders to integrate. However, in your world, which is trying to integrate, you have too often denied your shadow side or, worse still, expressed it through war and other collective acts of hatred.

An integrated society also will have the feminine and masculine qualities integrated. Both the masculine and feminine will be revered and balanced within the individual and within society. This will lead to compassionate (feminine) action (masculine) and intuitively guided (feminine) reason (masculine). Today your world is learning to value the feminine. Tomorrow's world will use the best qualities of both the masculine and the feminine to build a balanced society. As you balance these polarities within you, they will become balanced within your societies.

An integrated society will be balanced in all respects. For instance, work will be balanced with rest or recreation, and time with family will be balanced with time with community. Moreover, time will be allotted for everything that is required for balance and health: fun, creativity, work, family, friends, community, rest, eating, intellectual stimulation, physical activity, and spirituality.

It is even possible to lead a balanced life today. You already recognize the need for these things and their need to be balanced. You just have to learn to balance them within yourselves and create a society that honors this. It is easy to blame society for your imbalances. But society can only be changed by the individuals who make it up, often by joining together, but nevertheless by individuals.

This is why a shift in consciousness is so important to integration. Only as a result of a shift in consciousness will you demand a more balanced lifestyle. When you, yourselves, change inside, society will change. What will change you? Besides the influx of higher energy that you are receiving, pain will. Pain will cause you to question your current lifestyle and look for new ways to organize your lives and rebuild your societies. So, pain serves you in your transition to an integrated world.

An integrated world will not bar people from fulfilling their potential; it will not erect barriers between people, either. An integrated society accepts all people and their differences, because it recognizes the value of differences, even ones that lead to mistakes.

An integrated society understands that suppressing the freedom to make mistakes—and a lack of compassion toward them—fuels the cycle of violence, whereas acceptance, compassion, and forgiveness fuel the cycle of love, the cornerstone of an integrated society. Love enables a society to be integrated. The process of integration is a process of learning to love, or learning to break the cycle of violence.

Forgiveness is an important tenet of an integrated society. You give lip service to it but don't truly practice it. If you did, there would be less violence and hatred. Instead, many follow the tenet of "an eye for and eye," which fuels the cycle of violence. Ironically, this is a religious tenet. But like many religious beliefs, it is a distortion. It is not based on love, so it cannot be part of the Creator's teachings.

In an integrated society, justice is served, but not at the expense of society. Society is not served by punishment based on retribution. Society is only served by justice, which teaches and heals the accused. Thus, an integrated society not only reforms its criminals, but forgives them and helps them to reconnect with their spiritual self. It recognizes the spirit even within the most depraved. This ability to see the spirit in everyone draws it out and enables it to blossom, thus breaking the cycle of violence.

Acceptance is another tenet of an integrated society. Forgiveness and acceptance go hand in hand. Acceptance is extended to every member of society, and forgiveness is extended to those who make mistakes. They are two forms of the same thing: love. In an integrated society, all people and all differences are accepted and valued. Differences are understood to contribute to society's evolution and richness, to its ability to survive and thrive in an ever-changing world. Where there is acceptance even great suffering can be endured, because acceptance extends not only to people but to life. People who accept other people also accept life and all that it entails.

Acceptance implies an acceptance even of evil. Evil still exists in an integrated society, but it is understood for what it is and is transformed through love, rather than combatted. Evil must exist in a society that operates through polarities, even in an integrated society. An integrated society has polarities, but they are balanced. For societies that do not operate through polarities, integration is not an issue, for there is nothing to integrate. But for Earth and for many other worlds, integration is a goal. Service-to-self planets are not devoid of the need to integrate, but they are focused on the negative pole. They represent one extreme, while the Pleiadians of the past, for instance, represent the other extreme, where the negative has been denied.

An integrated society also is integrated racially. Love, acceptance, and forgiveness make it possible to adjust to racial differences. This is what will make it possible for you to adjust to your racial differences and the different extraterrestrials who will share your planet. Without a rise in consciousness, this would be impossible. This is why it may be inconceivable to you now that people and extraterrestrials could coexist without problems. There will be problems similar to your current racial strife, initially, but you will learn to live in peace.

The positives will teach you about peace, uplift your consciousness, and grant you many other favors. For these gifts, you will be willing to love and accept them. They will teach you how you and your neighbors, including neighboring countries, can benefit each other and live peaceably. They will appeal to your self-interest in teaching you about love. This will break the barriers between the people on Earth and pave the way for you to learn to love more unconditionally.

These barriers are not as difficult to break as you might think. Much of your pain and the violence and hatred it has produced is caused by ignorance. You have been blaming each other for your own ignorance, your own poor decisions. Once you learn to make better choices and organize your lives better, you will not find it so hard to get along with each other. When life stops going so badly, you will find it much easier to love one another. The positives will teach you what you need to overcome much of your self-induced pain.

11

THE FUTURE

You are about to become active members of the Confederation. You have always belonged, but you haven't had an ambassador. The Confederation is a group of individuals from various planets in this quadrant of the universe who monitor the activities on those planets. They are similar to the individuals on *Star Trek's* Starship Enterprise. This television program is not as farfetched as you might think. It is as natural to have a group policing an area of the universe as an area of the globe. And like the television program, the Confederation does not use force or violence or interfere unnecessarily in the affairs of the planets in their jurisdiction.

How did a television show come to reflect reality so closely? This is just one example of how you are being prepared to discover your interplanetary birthright. Confederation members and others are preparing you for this by planting creative seeds in the subconscious minds of television writers and others. This is done as a matter of course by spirit guides and others guiding your planet. The same thing is happening to your guides: they are being guided by others more evolved than they are. This is just how the universe works. It is a hierarchy, but a benevolent one that operates primarily for service.

You are being prepared to meet extraterrestrials in many other ways as well. Many science fiction writers, channels, and abductees have written about their experiences with extraterrestrials. And groups of Star People and Walk-ins have united to wake people up and tell them of Earth's interplanetary role.

You are being prepared less obviously as well, particularly through your dreams. Many of you have been visiting other planets in your astral body while you sleep. Artists have painted what they have seen during their nocturnal journeys, and musicians have reproduced the music of these realms. On some level, you remember these visits and will be able sometime to recall at least the joy and wonder you have felt on these travels. Your experiences on these flights are beautiful, joyful, and expansive. So, on a deep level, you already know yourself as an interplanetary being.

During sleep, many of you also go to what amounts to lecture halls, where you are taught the mysteries of the universe. Some of this information remains on the tip of your consciousness. When it is triggered by artists, musicians, science fiction writers, channels, and others, you resonate with it. You may even express this knowledge in your own poems, short stories, movies, musical compositions, and drawings. There are many signs all around you of your interplanetary heritage, because many are bearing witness to this now.

You are approaching one of the most important events a planet ever faces: a meeting with your creators. Throughout the universe, planets like yours have been seeded, nurtured, and then left to develop. Then, sometime in their evolution, the creators introduce themselves. That time is fast approaching for you. You are going to meet your creators, because they are about to take you to the next step: fourth density. This is always a momentous step in humanoid evolution.

That is why you are being visited now. So let's look at what this means to you and your planet to be moving into fourth density.

How do third-density bodies make this transition to fourth density? Some people won't be able to make the transition without dying and some will. Those who cannot handle the vibrations of fourth density won't be able to remain in their body when Earth shifts to fourth density.

Earth is shifting gradually rather than instantly, although not as gradually as usual. This will allow many of you to adjust to the higher vibration of energy infusing your planet. Those of you who can incorporate this energy into your body and raise its vibration may not have to shed your body when Earth moves into fourth density.

Those of you who cannot raise your vibration will have to leave Earth when its vibrations are no longer compatible with yours. For some, this will mean dying at the normal time. For others, it will mean leaving the body prematurely through any number of means, such as natural disasters, diseases like AIDS and cancer, epidemics, or famine. Be careful not to assume that those leaving in these ways are not good enough to remain. Such judgments will only set you back in your evolution.

Only a small number of people will make the transition to fourth density with their bodies intact. Others will still be able to return to Earth, but only after they die first. This is because, despite a consciousness compatible with fourth density, their bodies may be too damaged or contaminated with toxins for their cells to transmute. So a person's consciousness may be beyond the consciousness of his or her body. When this happens, the body has to be shed and a new one taken on before going on to fourth density.

Because of the difficulty of transitioning from third to fourth density in the same body, many will be leaving the planet in the next decade. Although this is tragic for those they leave behind, it is not tragic for their souls. They will be freed to go on to either another third-density planet or return to Earth later. The next decade will be a time for remembering and affirming your immortality, for anyone who clings to life too dearly will suffer. Death is just a transition, and a welcome one for many.

You will have to redesign your spiritual beliefs if you are to use the trials ahead as a springboard to higher consciousness rather than a cause to be bitter. What you believe will be exceedingly important during these times. Spiritual teachers who can help people see tragedy from a higher perspective will be in demand. As a result, reincarnation will finally be accepted across the globe.

As we said, the transition to fourth density will not happen overnight. The planet itself is making this transition more quickly than those on it. Its vibration is activating their shift. Some of the stress your civilization as a whole is feeling is due to living on a planet whose vibration is heightened. This is creating dissonance within people's bodies and sometimes resulting in disease. The bodies most affected by this are those that are polluted, stressed, blocked, or of a lower vibration. This makes it all the more important to eat well, meditate, and live healthily.

Seeing to it that your food is high quality and chemical-free is essential during these times. Now, more than ever, you need the help of healthy food and a healthy environment. Since few of you are eating well and living in unpolluted environments, healers are in more demand than ever before. Many, many healers have reincarnated from other planets and dimensions to help you heal yourselves and your planet so that you can make the transition to fourth density more gracefully. If your food and environment were more healthy, this would not be necessary.

Healing will be a major theme over the next decade, not only the healing of your bodies but of your social systems. Social systems are breaking down all over the world, not only in the United States. This will force you to reevaluate what you are doing. The United States will remedy its problems if it can get its democratic system functioning as it was intended to. Democracy has the flexibility to address the current needs and weather the changes ahead.

This decade and beyond will be a time of crisis on Earth. A purging is occurring, which will lead to a better world for all. This better world is a fourth-density world, and the purging is part of the transition to fourth density. All worlds experience some cataclysms during a transition to a new density. How severe these are depends on how rapidly the transition is made. Yours is being made very rapidly.

The crises you are likely to see have all been predicted before by seers like Nostradamus and Edgar Cayce: pole shift, volcanic activity, earthquakes, floods, droughts, pestilence, disease, and famine. You are already experiencing these, but on a lesser scale than in the future. The pole shift will be the most dramatic of these changes, but just how dramatic remains to be seen. Whether it will be a shift in the poles' location or a direct reversal is uncertain; either is possible. In any event, this alone will change the world's climate, which is already being affected by pollution.

We don't see these crises occurring all at once, but intermittently across the globe. Some areas will be hit harder than others. Where these will be is hard to predict, with some exceptions. The lands surrounding the Pacific rim will be altered by volcanic activity and earthquakes. The populations of Africa and India will be decimated by famine and disease. The United States will have droughts, as will the Soviet Republics. Beyond this, we cannot make predictions. We caution you about accepting predictions for the times ahead, since the many variables and changing conditions make prediction nearly impossible.

Over the next decade, many people will lose their lives and many of the children being born will not survive. Of those that do, many won't be able to reproduce unless you take drastic measures to clean up your environment now. You don't know what effect your chemicals and pollution will have on future generations. You won't realize the damage you have caused to people's reproductive systems until the coming generations are older. By then, it will be too late, and you will be struggling to maintain your numbers. You are seeing some signs of this in the increase in low birth weight babies, miscarriages, and couples unable to have children. This trend will continue unless you do something about the toxins in your environment.

The biggest change you will see over the next two decades is a change in population. Twenty-first century Earth will be much less populated. This will mean a renewal of the plant and animal kingdoms, with some lost habitats being regained. However, many plants and animals of the twenty-first century and beyond will be different from those today, because of adaptations to a changing environment and mutations resulting from toxins. So, the flora and fauna on fourth-density Earth will not look exactly like the flora and fauna on third-density Earth. This also will be due to the change in vibration. Some of your flora and fauna will not be suited to fourth density, and other forms will take their place.

Fourth-density worlds do not look exactly like third-density worlds, although they seem as solid to those who inhabit them as your world seems to you. Fourth-density worlds have a different matrix and therefore slightly different life forms, but ones you would still recognize as plants and animals. Fourth-density worlds also are brighter and more light-filled, which is the most obvious difference.

Since the transition to fourth density will be continuing at least throughout the twenty-first century, and your world will not be considered a mature fourth-density world until sometime after that, the description of fourth density that follows applies more to Earth beyond the twenty-first century than to the near future. Even so, the twenty-first century will be perceptibly different from the twentieth. Over the next century, those living will gradually come to experience their world differently. Their world will change with each passing year until eventually they will be living in fourth density.

Fourth density is difficult to describe, since it is unlike your world in so many essential ways. However, we will try to describe features of it so that you have a sense of what you have to look forward to.

Compared to third-density Earth, fourth-density Earth will be a paradise. Because of the presence of more light — not sunlight, but ethereal light — fourth-density worlds are blessed with lush, abundant flora and infinitely diverse fauna. Fourth-density people have learned to live in harmony with their surroundings, so fourth-density life will be lived close to and in cooperation with the Earth. In fourth density, animals cooperate with people and pose no threat to them. Fourth-density people are the masters of nature, but they are its servants as well.

In fourth density, cooperation exists between people just as it does between nature and humankind. There, people have a sense of belonging to something greater than themselves — to All That Is. They consciously align themselves with That. As a result, their cities and social structures are designed to benefit the social group, not just one person or group of persons.

In most fourth-density worlds, everyone's basic needs are met with minimal effort because of advanced technology. For example, food is abundant and provided lovingly by those who choose this occupation. Everything in society is provided out of love, not out of the need to earn a living. All functions within society are performed with joy. If someone cannot contribute to society for a time, he or she is gladly provided for by others.

Fourth-density worlds are the way they are, because people's consciousnesses are aligned with the Creator. This is what makes these worlds a paradise. People have always hoped that paradise was possible, and it is. However, this paradise is not the endpoint of evolution, but the beginning of one's service to the Creator.

Once you have moved beyond third density and received training as a guide, you are allowed to serve third density. Then you become spirit guides for those in third density. Some of you reading this have spirit guides from fourth density, although in nearly every case you also have spirit guides from fifth density. Some of you also have sixth and seventh density beings involved with you from time to time.

Fourth-density beings are invisible to third-density beings. This is confusing in thinking about Earth moving from third to fourth density. Will some of you be invisible to others? This transition will be made slowly enough that those alive, those who can accommodate the heightened vibrations, will gradually be transformed to fourth density. Since this will be happening to everyone on Earth at the same time, everyone will be a similar vibration and therefore visible to each other. You could think of the twenty-first century as a time of intermediate density: density three-and-a-half, changing to fourth. Beings of fourth density also will be visible to those transitioning to fourth density. Those transitioning would be considered fourth-density, even though they are more like three and a half.

Fourth-density beings are virtually free of disease and illness. They rarely fall ill, and what difficulties they do have can usually be remedied by advanced technology and medicine. As in third density, illness arises when people fall out of alignment with the Creator. When this happens in fourth density, the cause is understood and, consequently, easily remedied.

With so much time and energy freed by not having to struggle with illness or survival, huge strides can be made intellectually, socially, and spiritually. Fourth-density beings spend most of their time exploring areas of interest and expanding themselves intellectually and spiritually. What they engage in relates to their spiritual goals, which relate to service. For them, there is no such thing as knowledge for knowledge's sake, only knowledge for service's sake. Fourth-density beings seek knowledge for its potential to improve the lives of others.

This emphasis on the intellect does not leave fourth-density beings' bodies neglected. They are so well-attuned to their physical selves that very little is needed to maintain their physical strength and well-being. They automatically eat and move in healthy ways. The activities they are likely to engage in stretch and renew their bodies, not strain or abuse them. They practice exercises like those in yoga as a matter of course, simply because the body needs them. They don't say to themselves: "I should exercise twenty minutes today." They move as they need to as naturally as you breathe or yawn. Providing for their bodies is a reflexive action, not a conscious one.

Fourth-density beings live in family units, but without the strict gender roles of your lifestyle. Each gender does what it does best and what it chooses to do. And since each person is aligned with the Creator, one person's desires do not conflict with another's.

We have come to the end of this exploration for now, but you are far from the end of your journey, which is just beginning. The attainment of fourth density is a graduation of sorts. You are graduating from a world of suffering to one of service and compassion, never to return to a third-density world unless you choose to. Other third-density worlds will continue to nourish third-density people who are learning the lessons you have just come through. You will be in a position to help these people, which is one reason for your experiences in third density.

Everything humankind experiences has a purpose; nothing is ever wasted. Every experience prepares you to serve others, for that is the primary activity in a universe founded on love. Your world hardly seems founded on love at times. And yet, those of you who meditate know that love is all there is. Your sense of love as the basis of all will increase in the times to come, and your society will reflect this new awareness. Your educational, political, economic, and social systems will all change accordingly. You will become wise to the wisdom of love.

This may sound utopian and idealistic. How can what we have said about the future Earth be true? How can you believe this when experience tells you that life is suffering? The only answer we have to this, my friends, is to say that the only way through the suffering of third-density Earth is faith in a better world and the will to create it. You have the power to create a world filled with love, even though you may doubt it.

You have the power to create the world of your dreams. With the help of others, you are succeeding at it every day. Every day, you are getting closer to this reality of greater love, peace, and prosperity. Do not doubt the power of your faith or your actions. Look around you, and you will see so many others like you who are working to create a new world amidst the old. Look into each other's eyes and recognize your oneness, and this will strengthen you. We are with you always, as are many, many others. We all are sending our love and encouragement to you. Blessings to you!

APPENDIX

AN EXPLANATION OF DENSITIES

"Densities" is a term more and more people are running across, usually in channeled material, because it is being used by channeled entities to describe their understanding of reality and the changing reality of Earth.

A density is similar to what you understand as a dimension or a plane. There are many densities, planes, or dimensions coexisting simultaneously in space. They operate independently and are generally invisible to each other, because each is of a different vibration, or atomic density. With training and energy, lower dimensions can become visible to higher dimensions. However, higher dimensions are invisible to lower dimensions except under circumstances that are considered paranormal.

Usually seven densities are named, although densities do not stop at seven. The third to seventh densities relate to humanoid evolution, with third density being the first stage. First and second density are reserved for minerals, plants, and animals. They are on a track of evolution unrelated to the human track.

Human beings will soon enter fourth density, at least those who are ready. The Earth is moving into fourth density, and will no longer support third-density life. So, anyone wanting to return to Earth in other incarnations will have to be fourth density.

In fourth density, you will still experience yourselves and Earth as physical, but you will no longer be visible to third-density beings, except when you choose. To third density, you would appear to have bodies of Light, but you could also step down your energy and appear solid to them. Fourth-density beings can materialize and dematerialize in and out of third density. But they are still considered physical.

All higher densities appear to lower densities as Light-beings, with densities beyond the fourth able to appear in whatever form they choose. Fourth-density beings are confined to their physical forms, as third-density beings are.

Like third density, fourth density operates through polarities, but negativity is much less. Physical needs are fewer and much easier to supply. In fourth density, growth still occurs from challenges, but the challenges are different from those of third density.

Fifth density coincides with the higher astral plane, or the plane where spirit guides reside. Fifth-density beings act as guides to third and fourth-density beings, just as sixth-density beings act as guides to them. Fourth-density beings also can act as guides to third-density beings, but only under supervision.

With each rise in density, there is a rise in understanding, wisdom, and love. And each density has its particular lessons and challenges, as well as tasks. The shift from third to fourth density is one of the more miraculous shifts, since suffering no longer exists beyond third density.

ABOUT THE AUTHOR

Gina Lake is an astrologer and conscious channel with a Master's degree in Counseling Psychology. She has been channeling since 1986 and practicing astrology since 1984. She uses astrology and the Tarot to help people understand themselves and their life purpose. Theodore, the mid-causal plane entity she channels and the author of her channeled books, writes about reincarnation, personal and planetary transformation, new age philosophy, consciousness, healing, and astrology. Gina also channels several Ascended Masters, including Sananda and Kuthumi. In addition to writing, she leads workshops and classes in which she channels Theodore.

About the Publisher and Logo ...

The name "Oughten" was revealed to the publisher fourteen years ago, after three weeks of meditation and contemplation. The combined effect of the letters carries a vibratory signature, signifying humanity's ascension on a planetary level.

The logo represents a new world rising from its former condition. The planet ascends from the darker to the lighter. Our experience of a dark and mysterious universe becomes transmuted by our planet's rising consciousness — glorious and spiritual. The grace of God transmutes the dross of the past into gold, as we leave all behind and ascend into the millennium.

Publisher's Comment ...

Our mission and purpose is to publish ascension books and complementary material for all peoples and all children worldwide.

We currently serve over twenty authors who have books, manuscripts, and numerous tapes in production. Our authors channel Sananda (Jesus), Ashtar, Archangel Michael, St. Germain, Archangel Ariel, Hilarion, Mother Mary, Kwan Yin, and other Ascended Masters. We are in the process of extending this information to all nations, through foreign translations. Oughten House Publications welcomes your support and association in this momentous and timely endeavor. We urge you to share this information with your friends and families, and to join our growing network of like-minded people. A reply card is included for your convenience. Blessings and peace be with you always.

OUGHTEN HOUSE PUBLICATIONS

Our imprint includes books in a variety of fields and disciplines which emphasize the rising planetary consciousness. Literature which relates to the ascension process is our primary line. We are also cultivating a line of thoughtful and beautifully illustrated children's books, which deal with spirituality, angels, mystical realms, and God, the Creator. Our third line of books deals with societal matters, personal growth, poetry, and publications on extraterrestrials.

The list that follows is only a sample of our current offerings. To obtain a complete catalog, contact us at the address shown at the back of this book.

Ascension Books & Books for the Rising Planetary Consciousness

The Crystal Stair: A Guide to the Ascension, by Eric Klein. — ISBN 1-880666-06-5, $12.95

An Ascension Handbook A practical, in-depth, how-to manual on the ascension process, by Tony Stubbs. — ISBN 1-880666-08-1, $11.95

Bridge Into Light: Your Connection to Spiritual Guidance A how-to book on meditating and channeling, by Pam and Fred Cameron. — ISBN 1-880666-07-3, $11.95

The Inner Door: *Channeled Discourses from the Ascended Masters on Self-Mastery and Ascension,* by Eric Klein.
Volume One: ISBN 1-880666-03-0, $14.50
Volume Two: ISBN 1-880666-16-2, $14.50

What Is Lightbody? Offers a twelve-level model for the ascension process, leading to the attainment of our Light Body. Recommended in *An Ascension Handbook*, this book gives many invocations, procedures, and potions to assist us on our journey home. Related tapes available. By Tashira Tachi-ren — ISBN 1-880666-25-1, $11.95 (*available first quarter, 1995*)

Lady From Atlantis Millenium after millenium, male rulers have repeatedly failed to bring peace to this planet. Now Ascended Lady Master Shar Dae returns to modern America, to pursue her goal of world peace and the ending of duality. By Robert V. Gerard — ISBN 1-880666-21-9, $12.95 (*available January 1994*)

Intuition by Design Increase your "Intuition Quotient" through the use of this book and its accompanying set of 36 cards. A valuable tool for applying your intuitive intelligence to all aspects of the decision-making process in your life, by Victor R. Beasley, Ph.D. — ISBN 1-880666-22-7, $21.95

Transformational Tools

We offer an ever-expanding selection of transformational tools to assist you in your journey back to mastery. These include books and tapes, with such titles as *The Thymus Chakra Handbook*, *Reality Maintenance 101*, *On Eagle's Wings*, *E.T. 101*, and a series of tapes by Tashira Tachi-ren. For information on these and other titles in this category, please call or write for our free catalog.

Children's Books and Tapes

Books and tapes in this category include titles such as *Nature Walk*, *Mary's Lullaby*, *Song of Gothar*, and *Bear Essentials of Love*. Although primarily intended for children and adults who interact with children, they speak to the "child" within us all. For a full list of titles in this category, please call or write for our free catalog.

Discourses & Channeled Material

Hear the voices and experience the energies of our authors, on companion tapes to *Bridge Into Light* and *The Extraterrestrial Vision*. In addition, we offer many tapes on other spiritual and metaphysical subjects, such as *Parallel Realities, Birthing the Era of God, The Feminine Aspect of God,* and *Preparation for Ascension.* They are listed and described in our free catalog. Write or call for your copy now!

Music Tapes

We carry many titles of spiritually-based music, including both vocal and instrumental types. They collectively comprise a cornucopia of moods and sounds. Create your own "ascension chamber" whenever you play them — at home or wherever your journey takes you. For a listing of available titles, call or write for our free catalog. A reply card is bound into this book for your convenience, or you may reach us at the location listed on page 191.

Other Ascension Tools and Materials

We distribute many other items to assist you on your spiritual path. They include Ascension Cards and titles such as *An Act of Faith, The P'taah Tapes, Earth's Birth Changes: St. Germain through Azena, The Angels of the Seven Rays,* and many more. Ask for our free catalog; we stand ready to serve you!

READER NETWORKING AND MAILING LIST

The ascension process presents itself as a new dimension and reality for many of us on Planet Earth. Oughten House Publications now stands in the midst of many Starseeds and Lightworkers who seek to know more. Thousands of people worldwide are reaching out to find others of like mind and to network with them.

You have the opportunity to stay informed and be on our networking mailing list. Send us the enclosed Information Reply Card or a letter. We will do our best to keep you and your network of friends up to date with ascension-related literature, materials, author tours, workshops, and channelings.

If you have a network database or small mailing list you would like to share, please send it along.

CATALOG REQUESTS AND BOOK ORDERS

Catalogs will gladly be sent upon request. Book orders must be prepaid: check, money order, international coupon, VISA, MasterCard, and Discover Card accepted. Include UPS shipping and handling as follows (no P.O. Boxes for UPS):

$0.00–$10.00	$3.50	**Overnight** additional $10.00
$10.01–$30.00	$4.50	**Two Day** additional $5.00
$30.01–$50.00	$5.50	**International orders**: add $2.00 to shipping costs
$50.01–$70.00	$6.50	**Rush Orders**: add $2.00 to shipping costs
$70.01–$90.00	$7.50	
$90.01 and up	$8.50	

Send orders to:

OUGHTEN HOUSE PUBLICATIONS

P.O. Box 2008
Livermore • California • 94551-2008 • USA
Phone (510) 447-2332
Fax (510) 447-2376

ATTENTION: BUSINESSES AND SCHOOLS!

OUGHTEN HOUSE books are available at quantity discounts with bulk purchases for educational, business, or sales promotional use. For details, please contact the publisher at the above address.